# RUNNING
### with
# MONSTERS

# RUNNING with MONSTERS

A MEMOIR

**BOB FORREST**

WITH MICHAEL ALBO

CROWN
ARCHETYPE
NEW YORK

All rights reserved.
Published in the United States by Crown Archetype,
an imprint of the Crown Publishing Group, a division
of Random House LLC, a Penguin Random House Company,
New York.
www.crownpublishing.com

Crown Archetype with colophon is a trademark
of Random House LLC.

Library of Congress Cataloging-in-Publication Data
Forrest, Bob, 1961–
Running with monsters : a memoir / Bob Forrest with Michael
Albo. — First edition.
1. Forrest, Bob, 1961– 2. Singers—United States—Biography.
3. Rock musicians—United States—Biography. 4. Drug addicts—
United States—Biography. 5. Ex-drug addicts—United States—
Biography. I. Albo, Michael. II. Title.

ML420.F736A3 2013
782.42166092—dc23
[B]
                           2013019969

ISBN 978-0-7704-3598-1
eISBN 978-0-7704-3599-8

Printed in the United States of America

*Book design by Maria Elias*
*Jacket design by Nupoor Gordon*
*Jacket photograph: © Piper Ferguson*

All photographs are courtesy of the author unless
otherwise credited.

10 9 8 7 6 5 4 3 2 1

First Edition

For Sam, you're the best thing that I've ever found. Thanks for putting up with me. Elvis, I love you! Elijah, I'm proud of you! And for addicts everywhere, please know that redemption is possible . . .

# RUNNING
## with
# MONSTERS

# BEFORE WE GET STARTED . . .

Who am I? That's a good question. I'm the guy with the horn-rimmed glasses and the hat that you've seen on VH1's popular TV show *Celebrity Rehab with Dr. Drew*. I'm also known in some circles as "the Junkie Whisperer." It's a title I worked hard to earn. I've helped addicts from all walks of life and have offered them support, encouragement, and guidance based on my own firsthand experiences as I navigated the stormy seas of my own drug and alcohol dependency. I know the pain and desperation of addiction from the years I spent wasted and from my many futile attempts to get sober. It's been a strange trip. I started out as a teenage drunkard from the Southern California suburbs and became a sidekick of the Red Hot Chili Peppers and, later, Dr. Drew Pinsky. Now here I am.

Last night, my wife, Sam, and I got into a little argument.

About what isn't important. It was just a typical married couple's squabble that quickly deteriorated into "You don't feed the dogs!" and "Well, I feel unappreciated." Blah blah blah. You get it. Everyone who has ever had a relationship has had those fights. I went into the den—what my precious two-year-old son, Elvis, calls "Daddy's room"—and I started to think. I thought about my life, what it means, and how I got to where I'm now at. This book has mind-fucked me about a lot of things. It hasn't been easy to write. In fact, it's been painful. It hurts to look back over my childhood; my young adulthood; the music career that I threw away; the friends who have come and gone; survivor's guilt; gossip; stupidity; genius; joy; my older son, Elijah; all the mistakes I made; all the people I have let down; and the drugs. Constantly the drugs. No matter what, always the drugs. I was bound to them forever, I believed. I was never going to stop. There was no way to stop. I had no desire to stop.

Drug addiction has changed since I was young. Back then, there were certain prerequisites for the lifestyle. You read authors like Jack Kerouac, William S. Burroughs, and Hunter S. Thompson. You listened to bands like the Velvet Underground and the *Sticky Fingers*–era Rolling Stones. You found out about this lifestyle through the popular culture. There were course requirements to become a drug addict. Of course, only a small percentage of the people who enrolled in those classes actually graduated to the addict life, but they were pretty well versed in what to expect by the time they took that first hit of heroin or cocaine.

But prescription drugs have become huge. Today's addict is fed a steady diet of these medications—which are often prescribed by doctors for so-called legitimate reasons. Later, maybe, these addicts might shift over to heroin because it's cheaper—and better—but modern-day addicts will often just stick with their prescribed medications and go from doctor to doctor to get more of what they need. OxyContin, Vicodin, Adderall. A whole palette of multicolored pills to bring you up or bring you down. But it's still the same old drug-addict life-style that I knew: the Big Hustle and the Endless Search.

However, I was fortunate enough to experience a miracle. I managed to stop using and my reward was a new life beyond what I or anyone who ever knew me could have envisioned in their wildest dreams. I write this foreword as a completely different and changed human being. My name is still Bob Forrest, but that's about it. I am square and middle-class, and I live in a tract house in the mundane San Fernando Valley. I am happily married and I have a young child. We go to the zoo and I almost fit in with all the other dads. When I meet parents at my son's preschool and shake their hands, I think to myself, *If they only knew. Oh, my God, if they only knew who I used to be.*

What you're about to read is the story they don't know. It may seem sensational and a little surreal, but that's just how it was. Hollywood has always been a crazy place, but it was particularly so in the 1980s and 1990s. If I'm a little fuzzy on the dates, I apologize. I tell time by album releases and popular music. Unless it's something particularly momentous, I mostly associate the events of my life with what was playing on the radio at the time. But even then, a lot of those years I spent in a walking stupor, so I still may be off a little. It wasn't like I kept notes. But I did keep it real. And I hope I've done that here.

—Bob Forrest
Encino, California, 2013

# HUCK FINN AT 120 DEGREES

For a long time, I was angry. Angry at life. Angry at people. Angry at the world. But I wasn't always like that. The early years of my childhood were ideal. I was like a modern-day Huckleberry Finn, but one whose footloose and carefree Mississippi River had been traded for the burning sun and decomposed granite sands of Southern California's desert basin.

I was raised in Palm Desert, California, an affluent sister city to the more famous Palm Springs in Riverside County's Coachella Valley. Back then, in the sixties, it was still semi-rural. There were vast stretches of unspoiled desert, alive with birds and reptiles, but in town, there were golf courses, tennis and basketball courts, and all the normal amenities of upscale California suburbia: restaurants, bars, shops, and markets. It was an idyllic place for a kid. There was always something to keep me occupied. I had my family around me, my mother and my father, my three sisters, and my aunts and uncles. There was always something going on and our house served as a base of operations for trips to the golf course, motorcycle rides, barbecues, and fishing trips with my dad. I couldn't have asked for a better childhood. I was the center of the family's attention and I felt loved. I had a lot of fun. I didn't know any better. It was an alcoholic household.

The mistake most people make when they conjure an image of the alcoholic household is that they picture it as dark and grim. That's not completely true. If there's one thing that most drunks—and addicts—love, it's music. They can't live without it. Music keeps the party alive. It keeps it going. The Forrests lived by that motto. In the family room was a huge console hi-fi, its cabinetry a work of art in dark, cherry-stained hardwood. At full volume, you could hear it down the street and the floor and walls of our home would vibrate with the sound pushed out of the speaker grilles. If I stood close enough to one of them, I could feel the air move with each stab of sound. In the den was another, equally big and beautiful stereo rig. Along with those, we kids each had smaller record players in our bedrooms to spin the latest 45s, as well as our little portable transistor radios to catch whatever made the charts on the local Top 40 AM radio stations.

KHJ "Boss Radio" had the wattage to blanket most of Southern California with the station's signal and featured the "Boss Jocks," all of whom delivered the hits in rapid-fire teenage patter. I may have been too young to decipher a lot of it, but I somehow sensed that what they were saying was cool. It helped that my sisters loved rock-and-roll music and through them, it became the day-to-day soundtrack for my little kiddie life.

My dad was Idris Forrest, but everyone knew him as Idie. He made a good living and worked out of downtown Los Angeles, where he ran his own sign business, Fudge Neon—named for some nebulous, long-forgotten reason—with his brothers. In those days, there was a huge chain of discount supermarkets called Thriftimart. The stores were ubiquitous throughout Southern California, and each one featured a forty-foot-tall red neon T perched on the roof. You could see those fire-crimson electric beacons from miles away. My dad's company had the contract to supply the Thriftimart chain with these signature pieces, and Fudge Neon built them and maintained them for the company's growing empire. Idie would take me with him when he would supervise the crews that installed and maintained them. I remember climbing up the iron ladder that ran up the middle of the T with him when I just a little kid. By the time I was ten, I knew how to bend the delicate glass tubing that held the neon gas that provided the eye-popping color in those signs. In the early sixties, neon advertising was a lucrative business, and it put the Forrest family solidly in the upper middle class and knocking at affluence's golden door.

While Idie was a fun guy, my mom, Helen, could be kind of a bitch. She was high-strung. Idie loved her, but I don't think she liked him at all. She believed she could have done better. Before Helen married Idie, she had dated future College Football Hall of Famer Bud Wilkinson, the head coach at the University of Oklahoma from 1947 to 1963. After Bud finished coaching the Sooners, he went on to get involved in Oklahoma Republican politics and was ABC's lead commentator for the network's college football coverage before he returned to the field and coached the St. Louis Cardinals for the 1978 and 1979 seasons. He had also served on John F. Kennedy's President's Council on Physical Fitness. Bud had an impressive résumé, I'll give him that. Helen followed his career, and I think she always resented that she'd missed out on being the wife of someone famous. I'm sure she blamed it all on my dad.

Because Fudge Neon was located in downtown Los Angeles, during the week, Idie stayed at the other house we owned in nearby Inglewood, and my mom, my three sisters, and I stayed in Palm Desert. But if there was a Dodgers, Lakers, or Rams game scheduled on the weekend, my mom would drive me out to Los Angeles, where my dad and I would catch the action at Dodger Stadium, the Coliseum, or the Forum and then head over to Chinatown for a feed at Hop Louie's Golden Pagoda, a rickety, templelike structure that served up Cantonese grub. There was always an old guy who wandered the haphazard Chinatown alleys and footways with a hurdy-gurdy and a flea-bitten squirrel monkey that would come and harass you for coins under the brightly colored paper lanterns that hung overhead. There were live-food markets stuffed to the rafters with turtles and frogs and fish writhing around in algae-coated tanks. It was like visiting another planet. We had nothing like it in Palm Desert. Best of all, I got to bond with my dad—in Palm Desert I was trapped in a house full of women. Though that had certain advantages. My sisters helped shaped my early musical tastes.

*And when I touch you I feel happy inside.*

"Come on, Bobby! Let's dance!" squealed my sister Jane as she picked me up and twirled me around the room. It was the most joyful sound I had ever heard and we both laughed and spun until we couldn't stand up. "It's the Beatles, Bobby!" She was in the grip of that fevered teen condition called Beatlemania and it was contagious. Rock-and-roll radio pumped out the music all day, but television hadn't really caught the rock wave yet.

That all changed on February 9, 1964. I was barely a toddler, but I remember the excitement. It was like Christmas, Halloween, and a birthday all wrapped into one as the whole family gathered around the TV set on a winter's night to enjoy the fine and wholesome variety programming brought directly into America's living rooms every Sunday by impresario Ed Sullivan. My sisters couldn't sit still. They bobbed and bounced as they sat on the deep-pile shag carpet as close to the big cabinet that housed the television screen as they could get.

Helen said, "You kids will ruin your eyes!"

The girls answered in unison, "Aw, Mom!"

Then it happened. Sullivan made a stiff introduction and then *they* appeared. *"Close your eyes and I'll kiss you, tomorrow I'll miss you."* And with that line, the Forrest living room exploded with girlish squeals and shrieks of delight. "They're beautiful!" said Jane, tears in her eyes. She grabbed me and bounced me in time with the music and my feet, with not many miles on them, tattooed the floor with each beat.

I'm not sure what Idie and Helen thought. It wasn't their music at all and it wasn't aimed at their generation, but they had their own thing with the music of an earlier era. Frank

Sinatra and Benny Goodman were particular favorites, and the twin stereos would blast those sounds at their weekend barbecues and get-togethers, where the adults would gather and mix cocktails. I tried to absorb it all. While I could appreciate those records, they didn't speak to me like rock and roll did.

At first, it was the Beatles. Then came the surf-and-car-culture music of the Beach Boys and the teen-protest, us-against-the-world posture of Sonny and Cher. My sisters were sold on rock and so was I.

Idie, fueled by his booze, could be a character. I was his little buddy. My dad loved to spend money as fast as he made it, and we did all right, especially me. I got what I wanted, mostly. I went to basketball camp every summer, and we had a boat that Idie would use to take me fishing or water-skiing at the Salton Sea. I'd be asleep, and he'd come into my room before the sun was up.

"Get up, Bobby!"

"What?" I'd say as I rubbed the sleep from my eyes.

"We're going fishing! C'mon, get dressed! Time's wasting!" he'd say as he clapped his hands for emphasis. I'd fumble with my clothes and we'd pile into the car and head to the Salton Sea, a vast body of water that had been created when the Colorado River jumped its banks during a heavy flood in the early twentieth century and filled an ancient lake bed. Since that time, evaporation, agricultural runoff, and the lake bed itself had given the waters an ever-increasing level of salinity. But there were fish in its salty depths. Corvina, mostly. It was a fun place. In the 1950s and 1960s the area around it had been developed as a resort and there was boating, swimming, hotels, and bars. Now, through years of neglect, it's nearly a ghost town and an environmental nightmare with huge seasonal fish die-offs and plagues of flies. But back then, with Idie, the Salton Sea was an ideal place for a kid to spend time with his old man.

Idie and Helen liked to drink. Idie especially. He was a naturally gregarious and energetic man, and under the influence he could be a handful. As a businessman and a father, he had to contend with the average day-to-day pressures of a job and a family. He dealt with it by drinking. Booze was his wonder tonic, the magic cure-all for whatever might ail a man. Drinking temporarily freed him from his worldly concerns, so it wasn't all bad, I guess. I was a just a kid, and to me, it seemed to make him happy. Idie noticed my interest in music and came home one day with a little plywood acoustic guitar. It didn't sound great, and its stiff steel strings rode high above the fretboard. I didn't even know how to tune it. I learned a few rudimentary chords from a Mel Bay instructional book, but I didn't become proficient. Where I shined was when I posed with my six-string machine gun as if I were Elvis or Johnny Cash. I adjusted the strap so that it hung low and cool like a weapon, and then I'd bend a knee and twitch a hip and become a six-year-old rock star, adored by the masses and the envy of my peers. I had a favorite song that inspired this routine: Roger Miller's "Dang Me." I loved the twang and Miller's goofy lyrics. I was obsessed with that song. I fancied I could sing, and I'd belt out Miller's comically guilt-ridden lyrics in the reedy voice of a prepubescent pipsqueak. Somehow, my act was a hit with family and friends.

"Bobby! Get your guitar and play that song! You know the one I mean!" Idie would say after he'd had a few at one of his barbecues. "Get a load of this kid," he'd say. I'd scramble to grab my instrument from my bedroom and stand front and center ringed by adults. I'd hit my pose and grab an E chord as best I could. Then I'd launch into a hip-shaking version of the song:

*Dang me, dang me, they oughta take a rope and hang me.*

When I'd finish the line, I'd mimic Miller's scat singing and drink in the laughter and applause. It was my first taste of show-business success.

I got a weird, little-kid thrill whenever Idie and Helen would come home late from a night at the local watering hole, the Del Rey. Mom would needle Dad and they'd get into it. Eventually, Idie would have enough and turn his attention to us kids. I could hear him dramatically stomp into my sisters' rooms and wake them up with a good-natured "What the hell's going on in here?" The girls would shriek and plead, "Dad, we're trying to sleep!" but Idie would launch into some nonsensical monologue liberally peppered with swear words. The girls hated it—and my sister Jane says this is the reason why she still can't sleep well—but it never failed to crack me up. I guess Idie's humor didn't translate well to the feminine mind.

As kindergarten loomed, my parents became concerned about the local school district and didn't particularly want me attending public school in Indio with a bunch of Mexican kids whose parents were farther down the social scale than they were. They thought I might do better with a Catholic school education, so Helen covered the furniture with old sheets to protect it from dust and boarded up the house to await our eventual return and we left to be with my dad in Inglewood, which, in those days, was white—and safe—as milk. Besides providing me with what they thought would be a better educa-tion, the move would also save my dad his three-hour commute to the desert to be with us on the weekends.

Idie didn't change once we were all living together full-time. He was a full-time character. I left the house to go to school one morning and was stopped dead in my tracks by what I saw in the driveway. There, already surrounded by the neigh-borhood kids, was a golden two-seat sports car. Maybe it was an MG. Maybe it was a Triumph. It was hard to tell since the front end had been reworked. There, in midroar, with a fixed, thousand-yard stare and a frozen tongue, was the skillfully pre-served head of what had once been a living, breathing African lion. It really was a testament to both the taxidermist's and the auto body worker's art. It had been painted gold to match the rest of the car. It was the weirdest fucking thing I had ever seen, but also the coolest. Idie had been out drinking the night before and overheard some guy who boasted about his custom car. Idie chatted him up and went out to the lot to have a look at it. After he saw the one-of-a-kind creation, and with several drinks in him, he had to have it, so he bought it on the spot. Helen wasn't happy about it.

"What the heck is that . . . thing?" she asked.

"Baby, it's custom. There isn't another one like it any-where!" he said.

"It's hideous," she said. "And it's impractical. There's only room for two in it."

"Well, we still have the station wagon for you to haul the kids in . . . but this has a real lion's head right on the front! I'll have to see if I can get a horn that roars."

"It's ridiculous," said Helen.

She may have hated it, but I dug it. The kids in the neighborhood were impressed and I basked in the reflected glory of being the son of the guy who had a car with a real lion's head on it. You didn't see stuff like that in sixties suburbia. Not in Inglewood. Not in Palm Desert, where our other house sat idle. Probably not anywhere. And it had a radio, which I was allowed to control whenever I'd ride with Dad. The hits never stopped. Thanks to the AM radio of the day, I was constantly exposed to a wide variety of music. For anybody who didn't experience it, Top 40 AM radio of the sixties and early seventies was like nothing that's followed since. Stations played the best of everything in every genre. You'd hear poppy British Invasion stuff followed by James Brown's haunted screams followed by some twangy Jerry Reed country followed by jangly California folk rock followed by Carole King followed by who knows what. And on and on it went for twenty-four hours a day, only broken by the staccato ads for Clearasil, Marlboro cigarettes, local auto dealers, and the rest of the things that teens and young adults couldn't live without. Now radio's dominated by format and you get the best of nothing . . . or you get talk. The commercials are pretty much the same.

But things started going wrong. Dad's business was collapsing fast. Neon advertising was in its death throes as cheaper and less delicate plastic signs began to take over the market. You know that line in 1967's *The Graduate,* where Dustin Hoffman is pulled aside and told the future is "just one word: plastics"? It turned out to be true. Plastic signs were the future and the future had arrived. Idie refused to—or couldn't—adapt to the reality of the times. We had to sell the Inglewood house and move into an apartment in nearby Culver City. It wasn't a bad place, by any stretch. It was upscale and roomy, but an apartment was a step down. At least we had the house in Palm Desert. Still, they managed to send me to Catholic schools like St. Frances X. Cabrini and St. Augustine, and that's where I had my first sense of the cultural power of rock music. Up until I was about eight, I just liked music because of the way it sounded. It wasn't anything I could specifically explain, but one day, in the after-school company of a friend named Jimmy Beeman, I began to grasp how the adult world was threatened by it. The day's burden of school behind me, I walked to Jimmy's house past the well-kept lawns and flower beds of our new neighborhood. Cradled carefully inside my windbreaker was a 45 rpm record. It was "Light My Fire," a cover of the Doors' hit by a blind Puerto Rican guitarist named José Feliciano. The record had become a hit and I was fascinated by its Latin feel and Feliciano's mastery of the guitar. I found Jimmy in his front yard.

"You *have* to hear this!" I said excitedly. We went into his front room, where his folks had a hi-fi system similar to the one my folks had back home. Big, wood, and loud. We turned it on and placed the record on the spindle. The smoky groove filled the room and Feliciano sang, his voice quavering, *"Girl, we couldn't get much higher."* Jimmy and I stood there, eyes closed while we bobbed our heads in time to the beat like a couple of cool street-corner hipsters . . . or at least as close to that as a couple of third graders could gin up. We were lost in the sound when—*scratch!* "What do you boys think you're doing?!?" Jimmy's mom demanded, and shook us back to reality. She had ripped the needle off the record.

"B-but, Mom!" Jimmy stammered. He was embarrassed, but I could tell by the look in his eyes that he was scared too.

That's when he pointed an accusatory finger at me and blurted out, "It's Bob's record, Mom!"

*What a little sellout,* I thought as Jimmy's mom turned her fury on me. "Bob Forrest! What makes you think it's okay to bring this trash into my home? I think it's time for you to go home." She shoved the record back in my hand and frog-marched me to the front door. She shoved me out onto the walkway and slammed the door behind me.

*That was crazy,* I thought, and walked home. I hoped she hadn't scratched the record when she grabbed it off the turntable. When I got home, Helen was there to greet me at the door. She wasn't happy. "Jimmy's mother just called," she said. "What were you thinking?" she demanded.

"It's just a record, Mom!"

"It is *not* just a record, mister! There are grown-up . . . *things* in that song that little boys shouldn't be hearing." She paused for a moment and I searched my brain for what, exactly, those things might be. "And that Jim Morrison and those Doors of his are very bad people!" she added. Now I was totally confused. I had seen the Doors on TV and I thought they were cool. It wasn't even a Doors record Jimmy and I had played. Not long after Jimmy's mom had her little living-room freak-out, I watched the 1968 World Series with Idie on television. Feliciano played the national anthem. Like his records, his performance had a distinct Latin flair and was just . . . cool. Hip. Idie didn't say anything. He didn't have to. The world was changing all around him, and there was nothing he could do to bring things back to the way they used to be. It was pretty clear that things weren't going to turn around in the neon advertising business. And so, after fighting against the tide, my dad realized the game was lost and decided to retire. He uprooted the clan and brought all of us back to Palm Desert for the country club life.

Although we still had the house, it was a weird situation and one I couldn't quite figure out. We didn't have money like we used to have and I was old enough to sense the change. We still managed to keep ourselves enrolled at the fancy Indian Wells Country Club, though. Idie had cooked some deal through which we kept our membership and could maintain the appearance of success, but I didn't realize what kind of bargain he had made. I found out. One day, when I was twelve or thirteen, I was out near the golf course with my friends when one of them asked, "Man, is that your dad?" He sounded horrified.

Before I could figure out what he was talking about, another of my friends chimed in with, "That *is* your dad!"

I turned and saw Idie ride up on a big, industrial lawn mower. He was dressed like a gardener. The other kids kind of chuckled. "Hi, Bobby! You and your friends having fun?" And then he drove off, pushing the rattling contraption back toward the fairway. "Your dad's the *gardener,* man!" teased one of my friends, and they all had a laugh. It was fucked up and I felt embarrassed. In one quick step, I went from being the son of the cool guy who ran his own business and had once owned car with a real lion's head to the spawn of the stumblebum groundskeeper. I looked around at my friends as they hooted. *What a bunch of spoiled brats,* I thought as I watched these shallow young desert princes. In that crystal-clear moment, I realized that I was just like them: an insufferable, overindulged punk. It was time to get used to a new reality. If it was a rude awakening for me, it must have been even harder for Idie. His drinking increased and his genial moods were sometimes replaced by others that left us kids baffled. Where he had once been tolerant, even indulgent, of our love for rock and roll, he grew ever more impatient with the music we loved.

Jane had just gotten a copy of the newest release by the Beatles, *Abbey Road*. We decided to listen to it on the big hi-fi in the living room. We bounced and bobbed to the sinuous groove as John Lennon sang about flat-tops, Ono sideboards, and spinal crackers on the album's opener, "Come Together." We kicked our shoes off and worked up static electricity as our socks rubbed against the deep pile of the carpet. Every now and then, one of us would playfully tag the other and release a sharp, brief shock.

"Ow! Quit it, Bobby!" squealed Jane.

Just then our fun was interrupted when the room went dead quiet. Jane and I stood there staring at each other. "What just happened?" We turned and saw Idie, solemn as a prosecuting attorney, gently lift *Abbey Road* from the turntable deck and place it back in the paper sleeve and then slide that into the cover that showed the former mop-tops as they crossed an English street. Jane and I looked at our dad, perplexed. He put the record down on top of the hi-fi cabinet and addressed us. It felt like we were in court. He cleared his throat and said, very calmly, "Don't listen to this goddamn jigaboo music in the living room, kids." Then he walked out of the room.

Jane picked up her record. "What's 'jigaboo music'?" I asked her. Idie had never kicked about the Beatles before. This was something new. How was "Come Together" any different from "Michelle"? They were both Beatles songs. To me, it was all rock and roll . . . and I liked it.

Jane explained, "It's not the Beatles, Bobby. It's what they represent." She took her record back into her room. I thought about what she said and fingered through my folks' records. Pictures of various bandleaders and singers were on the jackets and all of them showed the men in suits and ties. Some of them even wore hats. The women were dolled up in haute couture, makeup perfect. The Beatles had ditched their matching suits several albums back. But Idie's reaction was more than just a criticism of fashion.

I couldn't articulate it at the time, but all the profound changes in American culture that had come in the wake of the Kennedy assassination—and more importantly, all the changes and reversals that had happened to Idie—were symbolized and crystallized by John, Paul, George, and Ringo and the band's evolving image. If there was a focal point of the cultural war and his own personal misfortune, it was these four young men from Liverpool. I understood what my sister had said: "It's not the Beatles, Bobby. It's what they represent."

I thought of the words of an earlier Beatles tune:

*You say you want a revolution.*

The battle lines had been drawn. My dad was on the side of what was old and in the way. I was a child foot soldier in the Army of Rock and Roll with all the changes it heralded. The new generation expressed its joys, outrages, and excesses through music. Its poets—Lennon, McCartney, Dylan—were saying things that mattered. And they were changing the culture; the signs were everywhere, in advertising jingles, television, and movies. It excited me, and that feeling only grew. Even the old guard fell under its sway. When Sammy Davis Jr., a member of Frank Sinatra's Rat Pack, showed up for the 1968 Academy Awards decked out in a velvet Nehru jacket and love beads, you knew who was winning the war. America had changed at its core and the Forrest family changed right along with it.

Now that I was in middle school, I reckoned if I could no longer be considered among the economically blessed, I could be among the reckless and dangerous. I could be an outlaw. It was no trouble to find other disaffected classmates. We were a bunch of little suburban troublemakers. Hoodlums in training. Our idea of fun was breaking into houses or gas stations. Not that theft was our thing. It was just fun to go where we weren't supposed to be. In those days, there wasn't the kind of security that you find now. It's not like we were master burglars. We were just dumb kids with a crowbar. I was the ringleader. I think I got the position because they all saw me as this tough kid from Los Angeles, someone who had been around and who was on his own a lot. A typical ruse for nighttime trouble was the old sleepover gambit.

"Hey, Mom," I'd say. "I'm going spend the night at Tommy Palletti's tonight."

"Okay, Bobby. Have fun," she'd say, and I'd be gone. It was pretty easy to pull off. None of our group's parents communicated much with each other, so nobody ever called to check. Besides Tommy Palletti, there was Scotty Simms and David Vaughan. We'd meet at the Indian Wells Country Club, the same place where Idie had his gardening gig, on the links after dark. Maybe there were some anger issues I subconsciously tried to work out, but the club was also a convenient and easy target. There were no security guards in those days. A golf course at night can be a great place to make mischief. We'd steal golf carts and hold demolition derbies. I learned that even if you're involved in petty crime, there is no way on earth to ever look cool in a golf cart. Of course, our pranks started to draw some attention. After one late-night spree during which several carts were wrecked, the local paper, the *Desert Sun,* had a front-page story with a headline that screamed, "Vandals Cause $5,000 Damage at Course."

I was at school when Tommy ran up to me holding a tattered copy of the *Desert Sun* in his hand. He shook with excitement. "Holy crap, man! Did you see this? They're talking about *us*! This is so cool!"

"You idiot! Shut up about that. If we talk about it and wave newspapers around, we're going to get caught. Do you want to go to juvie?"

"Juvie" was a place no kid wanted to go, even if it would validate that you were a genuine little teenage outlaw. I figured we had better cool our activities at Indian Wells. There'd be no more golf cart bumper cars at night for a while. But that was okay and didn't faze any of us too much. We lived out in the desert. There was always something to do. We found a new, more dangerous pursuit. Not far from where we lived was a wash that cut through the desert hardpan. When the flash floods would come from the summer monsoons and the usual winter rains, it shunted off the water. Mostly, though, the wash stayed dry. Miles Avenue cut across it and there was an overpass that provided a perfect place to hide, especially at night. It became our new place to meet. Back in those days, before people became concerned about the environment, the desert was seen as one big wasteland. Have old tires? Old furniture? Rusted-out appliances? Don't haul them to the dump. You have the world's biggest dump right out your back door. With a little bit of effort, there was no limit to what a group of enterprising, socially maladjusted kids could find if they didn't mind a little hiking. Old tires were the big prize to us. We'd find one and kick it hard several times.

"Never just pick them up," said David Vaughan.

"Yeah, man," said Tommy Palletti. "There could be a rattler or a nest of scorpions hiding in there."

You had to be careful when you played in the desert. Just about everything out there had evolved to cause damage. We kids were no different. We liked to break stuff. After we'd find a tire, we'd roll it back to the bridge near Miles Avenue. There, hidden by darkness and the structure itself, we would watch for auto or truck headlights as they approached.

"Here comes one!" Tommy said in a loud whisper.

"Sounds like a Beetle," David said as we all listened to the low and distinctive chug of that ubiquitous sixties car.

I'd watch the lights approach and calculate the car's speed against that of a well-pushed tire. When the moment was right, I'd hiss, "Bombs away!" and send the rubber juggernaut on a collision course with the approaching vehicle. We never caused an accident or any injuries, but sometimes there were dents and broken headlights. If we connected, we'd fall back under the bridge and suppress fits of laughter while the perplexed motorist would pull to the shoulder and inspect his vehicle. We'd especially get off if the driver knew the score and yelled something into the darkness. "As soon as I get home, I'm calling the police, ya little turds!" They were fun times for me. I remained leader of our little crew until another city boy arrived in town.

His name was Forrest too, only that was his first name. He was the son of a recently hired DJ at the local radio station. He had been around too. First in New York and then San Francisco. He claimed his father had written the 1950s song "Earth Angel." I have my doubts, but it was a good story and it gave him some credibility. He was a sharp kid too. He knew that if he wanted to call the shots in our little group, he'd need to let us all know who was boss. It took him about two days to come up with a simple but effective plan. It didn't involve much beyond kicking my ass after school. He did a thorough job and left me a battered mess. There was a new boss in town. I knew that I couldn't beat him in a fight, so I did the next smartest thing. I ingratiated myself with him. We became buddies. It's good to be number one, but if you can't have that, you might as well be second in command. Forrest and Forrest. Mayhem Incorporated. It was all a lot of fun, but I couldn't stay out every night. Things would get lively at home sometimes with Idie and Helen's drunken feuding and fussing, but I had an out. I'd escape and find week-end sanctuary with my eldest sister, Jane, who, by this time, had left home to live with her husband, Larry, a couple hours' drive away in suburban Whittier, California. She and Larry were good, normal people, and their house was a nice change from mine, where Idie played gardener and drank and Helen didn't know what to do except pick at him and wind him up. A lot of the time, my sister Susan acted as my surrogate mother out there in the desert. Our other sister, Nancy, could be a real handful. Unreliable. Selfish. Manipulative. Always a party person. Very beautiful, but very wild.

It was Christmas when I stumbled upon some interesting family history. I was twelve years old and I had been staying with Jane and Larry in Whittier, and we had all gone to one of my uncles' house to celebrate the holidays. It just sort of slipped out. My uncle was sitting at the bar in his living room and had tippled maybe a little too much. He was talkative. He put a hand on my shoulder and asked, "So, you've been staying with your auntie Jane, huh?"

*How drunk is this guy?* I wondered. I answered back, "She's not my aunt. She's my sister." I thought I had scored some points with that response, but then I noticed a tense silence had fallen on the room and I saw the looks everybody was shooting my uncle. I knew something was up. Something I wasn't part of or supposed to know. "Okay, so what's going on?" I demanded.

Jane and Nancy hustled me into the bathroom to have a little talk. The three of us huddled in there for an uncomfortable moment before Nancy just came out with it. "Bobby, I'm your mother."

That was heavy.

I'm sure I suspected something like that. I had heard my mom talk about the hysterectomy she had before I was born. I didn't know what it meant, but I knew how to use a dictionary. I had looked up the word. Whoa. *How could she have had me?* I wondered, but I didn't think too hard about it. Maybe there was some other way children were born that I didn't know about. It hadn't been much of a concern for me until this moment. I didn't know what to say to Nancy when she dropped the news on me. She and Jane watched me and waited for my reaction. I turned to Jane and said, "I wanted you to be my mom."

Nancy's lip started to quiver. She put a hand to her mouth and bolted from the bathroom. I stood there alone with Jane and hoped for an explanation. "Bobby, we've all done the best we could. It was a difficult situation, and, someday, you'll understand." Tears pooled in her eyes. "We all love you."

I just stood there, stunned. It was a Christmas I knew I'd always remember. Jane patted me on the back and said, "Let's go back out there and join the party." Everybody else seemed to carry on as if nothing had happened. Nancy and Jane pulled themselves together and my uncles freshened their drinks. I tried to tell myself nothing had really changed, but I suddenly felt like I was in a room full of strangers.

It was definitely weird, but that's just how people did things back in those days. People covered up and hid things. Family secrets. Secrets from the neighbors. Nobody questioned things, even the most obvious. People didn't want to pry too much in those days, I think. It was probably easier that way. When Nancy got pregnant with me, Idie and Helen shipped her off to St. Anne's, a charitable social services agency run by the Franciscan Sisters of the Sacred Heart. St. Anne's, which first opened its doors in 1908, was where Catholic families sent their pregnant teenage daughters to do penance for their promiscuity. There, on North Occidental Street in the Echo Park neighborhood of Los Angeles, they could carry their children to term hidden away from the world. Idie would visit Nancy on the weekends and they'd take occasional trips to the Echo Park lake, where he'd paddle her around in one of the little rowboats that were available for rent.

Nancy, I found out later, had a terrible delivery. She was in labor for two days and her pelvic bones cracked when I pushed through. Idie and Helen decided to adopt me and brought me home. Even after the Christmas revelation, I still considered Idie to be my real dad. I never met my biological father—and

I've never wanted to. Oh, I know his name and his story, but he doesn't matter to me. He's never been a part of my life and he never will be.

Idie provided me with as good a childhood as possible, but it was getting tougher for him all the time. By the time I was fifteen, I was getting unruly, and he was retired and not able to generate much income. He decided to sell the Palm Desert house and move us into a mobile home. To this day, I think it was an unbelievably dumb move. How much could the mortgage have been on that desert house? A hundred and fifteen dollars a month? So we continued our steady journey down the economic ladder. Still, Idie kept going. He continued to drink hard, but it, and his age, began to catch up to him. Doctors said he needed heart surgery. Helen gave me the news. "Bobby, your dad has to go into the hospital and have an operation."

*Okay,* I thought. It sounded serious, but doctors know what they're doing, so everything would be all right. I was wrong. Idie went in, but he didn't come out the same. He idled for a few months in a zombielike state. He wasn't the vivacious, exciting dad I'd grown up with. He was just another old guy in a hospital gown now. Then one day he died. I was shocked. He was gone. The seed of anger started to take root. *What kind of life is this?* I wondered. *How can the one guy I cared about and loved suffer all this shit? How could he lose his business, go broke, and then be gone in an instant? Is this all there is to look forward to?* I was fifteen, and it wasn't fair, it wasn't right, and there wasn't anything I could do about it.

Idie had given me a lot of his personality. I must have absorbed it through osmosis. Like him, I could never handle the nine-to-five routine. The old man was all over the place and strictly in the moment. I was just like him. Now I was on my own and left to my own devices. I raised myself from then on. I took up Idie's favorite pastime and became a big fan of Bacardi 151 rum mixed with cola. I'd sneak it from the liquor cabinet. Helen never noticed. The raw alcohol taste of the rum took some getting used to, but mixed with enough cola, I could by-pass the gag reflex. I loved to feel the warmth of the booze heat my innards and spread to my arms and legs. Even better was the way it made my head feel. I could achieve some degree of peace and satisfaction. I felt complete. Confident. It was a magical elixir. Some kids in my class thought Wheaties were the break-fast of champions. I knew different. Getting a buzz on before I left the house made school more interesting. I could talk to girls and I discovered they liked the bad boys. I was this wild desert kid. I lived for cigarettes, booze, dirt bikes, and trouble. These rebellious skills would serve me well when I started my rock-and-roll band as an adult. But I also discovered Jack Ker-ouac and his philosophy, which urged a sort of mad love for life. I adopted that as my creed. *Be mad for living,* I thought. *Always.* I mean, what other choices did I have? I was on my own and I was pissed off.

Punk rock entered the picture. If ever there was a style of music that reflected what I felt at the age of fifteen, it was punk. I didn't know much about it, but I became obsessed with it. You have to remember that back then, there was no Internet, no cable TV with hundreds of channels, and no twenty-four-hour entertainment news cycle. If you followed music, you got your news through the radio or *Rolling Stone* and *Creem* maga-zines. *Rolling Stone* came out every other week, and *Creem* was a monthly publication. The quest to keep current had to be done from street level, so you combed the record stores and you tried to go to shows. At fifteen or sixteen I was in a record shop every day. I had enough musical sense to be able to draw parallels between Elvis Costello and Bob Dylan. I understood that Tom Petty and the Heartbreakers were like the Rolling Stones. I heard the Ramones and recognized they were a Phil Spector girl group at their core. The new music was not unfamiliar to my ears.

But I kept reading about these other bands in the music magazines. The Sex Pistols, the Dead Boys, the Damned. What the fuck were they all about? The record stores I went into didn't have any of that music yet. Being a completely obsessed music geek, I would go in and bug the clerks.

"You got the Sex Pistols yet?"

"No, kid. It's on order."

"What about the Damned?"

"Nope."

"Dead Boys?"

"Who?"

"When's the Sex Pistols' record going to get here?"

"Soon. Look, kid, why don't you check out the new Peter Frampton album?"

I was frustrated. But one day, a Sex Pistols record finally arrived. I walked out of the store with my latest purchase, a twelve-inch single of "Anarchy in the UK" backed with "I Wanna Be Me." I hurried home and went straight to my room to put it on the turntable. I played the B-side first and was floored. *This is it! This is fucking revolutionary! These guys are the new Beatles.* I played the record a few more times. What I heard felt so important that I went into the bathroom and cut off my long hair with a pair of scissors. The hippie era was dead. Punk rock was here. I needed more.

The records began coming into the stores. Next came the robot-riot sound of Devo. That was followed by the Clash's rock-meets-reggae underclass anthems. This stuff was like a tidal wave that washed over me. It even affected my musical heroes. I had recently seen Iggy Pop perform on *The Dinah Shore Show,* an afternoon talk and variety program hosted by the aging big-band singer. I couldn't believe it. David Bowie played keyboards in Iggy's band. I had been obsessed with Bowie since his ultra-flamboyant Ziggy Stardust days, and here he was looking subdued and anonymous as he pounded the keys while Iggy sang "Funtime." When I saw that Iggy was scheduled to play some shows in Southern California, I had to go.

The Golden Bear was a tiny little club in Huntington Beach that sat across the street from the city's famous pier on the Pacific Coast Highway. I pushed myself inside for the show. I was a little disappointed that the club was so small that Bowie had decided not to show for the gig. It didn't matter. The energy was high wattage. You could feel it as soon as you were inside. There was an opening act. A punk rock band from right in town. I think they called themselves the Crowd. Huntington Beach boys. They probably had only been together for a few weeks, but their rough edges weren't a drawback. With the first blast from the kick drum, the crowd exploded in this weird up-and-down dance I found out was called the pogo. The energy was unbelievable. Punk rock was great on records, but it couldn't be fully understood unless it was heard live. Preferably as close to the stage as you could get while being slammed and jostled by dancing kids. I was amazed by the girls too. Punk rock girls were badass. They had wild haircuts and didn't wear underwear. I was sold.

After that first show I saw at the Golden Bear, I couldn't stay away. I saw the Ramones. It was the most energetic show I had ever seen. Bodies bounced and the music pulsed. Then I started to catch the Los Angeles bands: the Circle Jerks, the Plugz, and anyone else from the big city. The important thing was to be there. By my senior year of high school, after a steady diet of Los Angeles–bred punk rock, I knew that was the town for me. I just had to figure out a way to get there.

# SCHOOL DAYS

By my senior year of high school, I was a smart-mouthed, music-obsessed kid who liked to read everything I could get my hands on. I also drank Bacardi rum for breakfast. Just your average, all-American teenager. I had left Palm Desert with Helen two years before and we shared an apartment in Huntington Beach, California, in Orange County, just south of Los Angeles. I was already enrolled at Golden West, a local community college, and took some classes there along with the last of my course work at Marina High School. Because it was a community college, anyone could enroll, and as a student at Golden West, I was allowed a stipend from Social Security. Five hundred dollars a month was a solid chunk of change for a seventeen-year-old kid like me and all I had to do to ensure it arrived in the mail was to remain affiliated with a college. It was my main hustle in those days.

That was a busy year for me. Along with school and rock-and-roll shows at the different clubs that stretched all the way from Orange County to L.A., I had also discovered speed, weed, and cocaine. Like any other teenage stoner, I was introduced to marijuana early. It was one of those things that was always around at high school parties, teen dances, wherever kids would meet. It was freely shared. "Do you get high?" was not an uncommon opening question when meeting new people in those days. No stranger to booze, weed didn't seem like a big step to me. Its effects were gentle, but it somehow seemed cooler. More rock and roll. Young. I liked the communal aspect of sharing a joint and as I traveled that circle, it was inevitable that I would come across stimulants. Pills, powders, and capsules. "Try this, Bob!" someone would say.

"What does it do?"

"It lets you keep going."

That was the truth. Those little tablets, a multihued rainbow, kept me going all night long and brought things into a sharp, focused perspective. They were just the thing for when the sloppy effects of booze threatened to end the party. Powdered bathtub crank, made by anonymous bathtub chemists, was just as good. A quick line snorted off the back of a hand or a dirty mirror was like a burst of electric energy. Cocaine was around too. It was more expensive than the other stuff, but it had its own mystique. In the seventies, it had come into its own and I was right there to snuffle it up whenever it was around.

But all these hobbies cost money. While I got $500 every month from Social Security after Idie's death, it hinged upon my being a student. And with my tastes and habits, I needed more dough. I was industrious and I liked money. I ended up working three jobs. Two was typical for a kid back then. I worked in a record store and I also had a job at a little pizza parlor where I tossed dough, slung sauce, and made deliveries. The third job found me at a carpet-cleaning enterprise that contracted with commercial real estate and kept the floors of banks and office buildings spotless. For a kid, I pulled in pretty good money. Of course, that can be a dangerous thing, and it went to my head. Helen still tended to think of me as a twelve-year-old child, and I chafed at the idea. The fact was that I made decent money and financed weekend trips to Las Vegas, I bought good drugs, and I generally did as I pleased. She tried to lay down the law one night in the kitchen.

"Bobby, you just can't do whatever you want. We have rules here."

I ignored her.

"Bobby, did you hear what I said?"

"No," I said as I shook some cornflakes into a bowl.

A tone of anger crept into her voice. "You need to show me some respect, young man!"

"I don't 'need' to do anything."

And then, for added emphasis, I took a plate from the rack and smashed it on the floor and stalked out of the kitchen and went to my room, where I slammed the door and cranked up the Clash on my stereo. It wasn't one of my finest moments. It was stupid and small, but it hurt her. And much more than I knew.

A few days later, Helen told me, "I can't live like this any-more." She retired. She was done. She packed up and left to live with her sisters in a retirement community on the edge of Los Angeles and I was on my own as a high school senior. The separation was good for us. Helen was free to enjoy her retirement and I learned fast about rent and responsibility. A two-bedroom apartment like ours, a block west of Beach Boulevard, the main drag through town, cost a steep—for then—$650 a month. I took on a roommate to help with expenses and keep solvent, but I was totally unprepared for what I had taken on. Even with the money I had coming in from work and Social Security—and the help I got from family as long as I did okay in school—I had no idea how to budget. I was lost emotionally and financially. If rent was due in four days and I only had $450, I'd immediately go out and spend $200 on cocaine and booze to feel better about the situation, but then I'd be even farther in the hole.

I took on an additional job. There was a nightclub in Costa Mesa called the Cuckoo's Nest that was a popular spot for surf punks from Orange County and rusticated hillbilly punks from landlocked San Bernardino County and the far eastern edge of Los Angeles County. The club shared a parking lot with a redneck bar called Zubie's and the local cops and beer-addled urban cowboys had no problems hassling the kids, who, naturally, pushed back. It was a fun place. Chaotic. I hung out a lot with a band called the Popsicles who were managed by Kim Fowley. They weren't quite punk and they weren't quite rock. In a lot of ways, the Popsicles were like a male version of Fowley's earlier group the Runaways. They were good-looking enough to be featured in *Teen Beat* magazine. If they're remembered at all now, it's for their cover of ABBA's "Tiger." You had to have some balls to cover ABBA in those days. It was a fun scene, and with pressure from the rent and my living situation in Huntington Beach, I decided to get smart and get out. As soon as school was over and I graduated from Marina High, I moved to a house in Costa Mesa, where I rented a room for $75 a month. A great burden had been lifted from my young shoulders. And I had a lot more money for drugs. That was good.

I stayed enrolled at Golden West College. One of my roommates, Dave Hansen, took courses there too. It was a sun-struck campus of low-slung buildings near the old grasshopper-like derricks that pumped the last drops of crude from the oil fields that spawned the area's 1920s oil boom. The school was close to the surf and had lovely, lovely coeds, tanned and ripe, like creatures straight out of a soda ad. It was like being in the middle of a Beach Boys song come to fleshly life. I enrolled in journalism courses and wrote for the school paper, the *Western Sun*. I covered the local music scene. One of the first things I wrote was a review of an AC/DC show at Anaheim Stadium. I was really proud of that.

During weekend excursions, I became fascinated with the Starwood Club, a sweaty, gritty little night spot near the corner of Santa Monica Boulevard and Crescent Heights Boulevard in Los Angeles. It was a great place. There was no telling what you could hear there from night to night. Lots of music. The place was managed by a guy named David Forest. He was one of those wildly flamboyant gay guys who long ago had given up caring whether anybody knew he was gay or not. It didn't matter in Hollywood. When I found out we shared a last name, I didn't waste any time in coming up what I thought was a slick hustle. Somebody would ask me, "Do you know David?"

"David Forest?" I'd reply.

"Yeah, man. The cat who runs this place. Nice fella. Flamingly gay."

"Oh, yeah. Of course I know him. He's my uncle." I'd flash my driver's license and show my name. Nobody ever noticed that we spelled our names differently. The ruse caught on. People accepted it as fact that I was David Forest's nephew. David even started to believe it. It gained me access. I never had to pay to get in the club. I had the magic pass. I saw so many free shows I lost count. I also gained access to David Forest's inner circle and was allowed into his office, where he'd hold court with his boy toys. Of course there were drugs. David would ceremoniously break out a bag of cocaine and say, "Oh, this is beautiful, boys. Look at how it sparkles! That's how you can tell if it's good. It catches the light like crushed pearls!" His coterie of rough trade and pretty boys would giggle and squeal with dramatic euphoria while David drew out huge lines on his desk and then brought out a sterling silver straw set with a small blue star sapphire. It was a fascinating scene to my increasingly opened eyes. I was also intrigued when I learned that the Starwood, along with several other area clubs I frequented, was owned by a reputed drug kingpin named Eddie Nash, a shadowy Palestinian with a spooky and dark reputation for violence and mayhem who would later be implicated in the grotesque "Wonderland Murders," which left four people beaten to the consistency of guava jelly in a Laurel Canyon duplex in 1981. To a kid from the OC, things like this were undeniably exciting. You could read about these events in the *Los Angeles Times,* but to walk the same streets as the people you read about was a wholly different experience. I loved it. I set my brain to figuring a way to move to the big city.

The first step was to get out of Orange County. To keep the Social Security money flowing, I transferred to Los Angeles City College in Hollywood. The second step was to find a place to live, and I found a great spot, one with a serious rock-music pedigree. Three blocks east of Main Street on Fifth Street downtown was a building that had a café and bar on the ground floor called the Hard Rock. It wasn't the fancy, upscale chain, but the place that inspired it: a wino-infested hole in the wall that had been featured on the back cover of the Doors' *Morrison Hotel* album. Upstairs was a huge loft that took up the entire third floor. It cost $600 a month, but it was a lot of space . . . *and it was over a place the Doors had made famous!* I couldn't believe it. I had learned my lesson about rent in Huntington Beach, so I enlisted some roommates. My friend Dave Hansen had a brother, a skinny kid named Chris who knew his way around the fretboard of a guitar. His punk rock name was, humorously, Chris Handsome. He came aboard along with his girlfriend, Lora Jansen, and my girl, Sheree La Puma. We were all under the influence of the punk scene, so we formed a band. It seemed like the right move. Lora played drums, Sheree handled key-boards, Chris and I played guitar, and I also sang. We weren't a standard rock group. We weren't even a standard punk band. We were an art-noise band. I had always had the ambition to play music, but I was convinced that it would have to be some-thing avant-garde and not mainstream because I thought of my-self as a weird-looking person and my chops on the guitar were average at best. I would never be a *Teen Beat* magazine cover boy like Shaun Cassidy. I'd never even be like the Popsicles and get featured on the *inside* of *Teen Beat*. It wasn't until I saw the Replacements do a show in 1983 that I thought, *Holy fuck! Really weird-looking, unattractive people can play rock music!* It was a revelation, but until then, I was firmly committed to noise rock. We managed to book a few gigs at Al's Bar, a small space on the ground floor of the American Hotel, a transient flophouse, that became known for hosting a lot of up-and-coming punk bands.

Despite the fun and the excitement of playing in a group, I had one primary mission: to keep the cash coming in. And the way to do that was to stay in school. Any school. It didn't really matter. Unlike Chris, who had real academic goals, I only cared about that monthly check, so I drank, did crystal meth, and used cocaine, all to the detriment of my studies. I loved the rock-and-roll party lifestyle and felt at home there. Drugs and alcohol were central to it. The Beatles, Dylan, and the Stones all endorsed drugs either outright or through their music, and it seemed to me that I was following some grand rock tradition. As a bonus, when I was high, I felt really good. I had fun. I was only at LACC for two semesters before I flunked out. The Social Security people contacted me.

"Mr. Forrest, we see you're not currently enrolled in classes at Los Angeles City College."

"No, no," I said with practiced nonchalance. "I've been accepted at Cornell University. You know, *the* Cornell University. That's why I'm not in those classes."

In the days before computers and the Internet, this kind of scam was incredibly easy to pull off. Records got lost all the time. The mail was slow. Any number of things before the advent of the Digital Age could slow things up or cause delays. And all you really needed was a little time to work the system. I had some family near Watkins Glen, New York, so I decided a short break from L.A. might be fun. An academic vacation of sorts. I took off for the East Coast with Sheree. I admit that I liked the prestige of being a Cornell undergraduate, even though, technically, I wasn't. In fact, I hadn't even bothered to apply. When I got to Watkins Glen, I went to the financial aid office on campus and put on a little show to keep the money coming in.

"I'm not even registered here? How can that be? I've come all the way here from Los Angeles, and now I'm stranded here? You have all my paperwork. I sent it in months ago!"

The poor clerk in the office looked stunned. "Well, this does happen from time to time. Here, let me get you started," she said, and handed me some forms to fill out.

I worked my hustle. I ran my hands through my hair in a pantomime of false despair. "This is so bad . . . so bad. What am I going to do? I just did this whole life-changing thing to move here. I left my home all the way across the country. My financial aid's been transferred here!" I looked upset. I looked like I was about to cry. I thought maybe it wouldn't be a bad idea if I enrolled in some drama courses. That stuff could come in handy down the line given my increasing reliance on putting on these kinds of shows.

I convinced her. She sighed and peered over the rims of her glasses. "Okay, okay," she said. "Now that we've started the paperwork, everything will be fine. You can register."

I signed up for classes. I skipped drama, but I took on a full load of art and history courses at one of the most prestigious colleges in the country. That alone felt like a huge accomplishment. Of course, my hustle didn't always work. This particular one only lasted for about a month. I had thought that once I had my foot in the door as a registered student, I'd just slip through the cracks and nobody would ever notice that I'd never even bothered to apply. They did notice.

In an art history class one day, the tweedy professor cleared his throat and said, "Mr. Forrest, may I speak to you?"

I gulped. "Sure." It didn't feel right.

"You can't attend this class. You need to go to the registrar's office."

I trudged over and went inside, my typical morning hangover suddenly, screechingly worse. The woman behind the desk sent me back to another office deeper in the building. A stern-looking official had my pathetically, laughably thin folder in front of him. "Mr. Forrest, we don't have transcripts from you. Nor do we have SAT scores, nor do we have a basic application form, nor do we—"

I cut him off. I tried to work up a front of righteous, middle-class indignation straight from the heart of suburbia. "This is outrageous!" I sputtered. "What kind of incompetent office do you run here?"

He just leaned back in his chair and said, "I'm sorry. You are not a student at this university."

Well, the jig was up. It was a good scam while it lasted. I turned around and headed back to Los Angeles and re-enrolled at LACC, which I was once again eligible to attend. Once I officially signed up for classes again, those government checks started to arrive in the mail. The purpose of my student days and my only academic goal was really just to be registered somewhere to get money to live and to do drugs and go to clubs. It was a pretty good hustle as far as hustles go.

Now that I was back in town and my financial situation was settled for the moment, I got back to my real business: rock and roll. One of my favorite clubs to visit was the Cathay de Grande. Situated dead center in Hollywood at the corner of Argyle Avenue and Selma Avenue, the club's main stage was the subterranean home to some of the most exciting music in Los Angeles. It featured the raw punk of local acts like Fear, X, the Circle Jerks, and countless others. The Orange County punk bands like Social Distortion made the Cathay their home away from home. The club was also home to a vibrant local roots-rock scene, with the Blasters and Los Lobos often taking the stage, as well as numerous cow-punk bands, who, really, were playing the kind of straight-up Bakersfield country that had fallen out of favor with rednecks but was finding a new audience with young punk rockers. It was the kind of music that would have fit right in at Zubie's in Orange County . . . if the sweaty cowboys could get past the punk rock look of the musicians playing it.

I worked that scene like it was a job. Sure, I partied and had lots of fun, but I constantly inserted myself into peoples' faces. I met the musicians, the regulars, and all the staff. I made sure to remember everybody's name. I sincerely liked just about everybody I met at the Cathay and I was genuinely happy to be there. People responded to that. I was a best friend to whoever I might meet. It wasn't long before I was accepted into the inner circle.

Things were great at the Cathay, but they could have been better according to the owner. There was a problem. The place was divided into two sections, upstairs and downstairs. Downstairs was where the bands played and where the crowd stayed. Upstairs there was a beautiful, ornate bar that was left over from the club's restaurant days. Very few of the customers used that bar. There was no draw upstairs. All the music and fun happened downstairs. The reluctance of the crowd to go up-stairs was costing the place currency. The major moneymaker at any club isn't the door, it's the bar. The owner, Michael Bren-nan, had an idea. "People won't leave the stage because they want to hear music. What if we have music upstairs?" I was twenty-one years old, loved rock and roll, and lived two blocks away. Michael approached me with his idea. "You're here every night anyway," he said. "You come in, play some records, and make a little money too." His logic was flawless, and the truth is that I would have carried out his plan for free if he had asked. I started coming in five nights a week with a crate of records to spin through the bar's sound system. I took care and consider-ation with what I picked to play. I had a vast collection of vinyl I had collected over the years that covered just about every genre of twentieth-century music. I'd play everything from scratchy Delta blues to early rock to psychedelia to the latest under-ground sounds from Europe. It worked. People started sitting at the bar because now it seemed like something was going on. People would come up, buy a drink, sit and talk and cool out, maybe buy another round or two, and then go back downstairs. I couldn't believe my luck. I was in the right place at the right time. The gig supplemented my student money. I got $15 a night and, equally important, I got all the booze I could drink on the house. Best of all, I was in the center of the action at one of the coolest clubs in Los Angeles.

One night, I was in the DJ booth playing "Defunkt" by De-funkt when this shirtless, hyper, rubber-faced kid barged his way in like some sort kind of punk rock commando, took the needle off the record, and flipped it over to put on "Strangling Me with Your Love."

"That's a better song!" he yelled at me before he ran out on the dance floor and started slamming around with the rest of the moshers. I was dumbstruck. It displayed a total lack of respect, although I had to admit, it was a pretty ballsy move on the kid's part.

"Who the fuck was that? Security! This kid just came in and flipped my record!" I yelled. The guards went looking for him, but he was a slippery little bastard. They couldn't catch him. And he kept doing it all night. I was impressed by his persistence—and his taste in music. Finally, I managed to get him to sit still long enough to tell him, "Look, man, you can't just come into my DJ booth and flip my records."

He looked at me like I was insane and laughed. "I'm Flea. I play bass for Fear!" he boasted. "I can do anything I want!"

Another regular was Lori Paterson, who eventually became my first wife. She helped book talent for Club Lingerie. She must have seen something in me and we started a fairly dysfunctional relationship right away. She was a little older than me and had absolutely no trouble matching me shot for shot and line for line when it came time to drink or get high. And it seemed like it was always the right time to indulge, although neither I nor anyone around me saw what we were doing as excessive or over the line. It was just something to do to keep the party in constant motion. I moved in with her and one day, fueled by booze and speed, we drove to Victorville in the high desert across the San Bernardino county line and tied the knot. She had faith in her man's talents and kept after her boss, a flamboyant Scotsman named Brendan Mullen, to let me DJ at the Lingerie. Whatever she said convinced him. I also grabbed a gig where I spun records at Eddie Nash's Seven Seas club. My schedule was full and I worked every night. From Lori's apartment in Beachwood Canyon, my nightly routine took shape. I'd wake up late. Drink, do drugs, and crate up the records I planned to use that night. I didn't have a car. I didn't need one. My days in Orange County had been spent on the deck of a skateboard, and I had a fine fishtail ride. Powered by gravity, I'd start at the top of the canyon, my crate of records cradled in my arms, and free-fall, high out of my mind, down to Gower to the Cathay de Grande. Sometimes, I'd slide onto Franklin, or I'd just highball it all the way down Beachwood to the Lingerie. You can build some frightening momentum on your way down that hill. If I was scheduled to work the Seven Seas, I'd hook onto Hollywood Boulevard. The stone paving that makes up the Walk of Fame is a fast surface and I could haul ass as I dodged pedestrians and balanced my records.

Now there was movement. My life had direction. I no longer felt the need to continue my charade with college. My real education had begun.

# LA LEYENDA

D rugs were everywhere in the eighties, and everybody I knew used them and loved them. Some were more devoted to the substances than others, but I didn't know anyone who ever passed up a drug when it appeared. "Hey, you want one of these pills?" someone would say as they pulled out a plastic sandwich bag stuffed full of multicolored capsules.

"Uh, what are those?"

"I don't know exactly. The red and yellow ones will slow you up and the brown and orange ones are some kind of speed."

"Well, pass 'em over, man. Pass 'em over! Got a beer to wash these down with?"

There was a dividing line, though, and that was the needle. You'll find, sometimes, that the most enthusiastic sniffer of medicinal powders will have a moment of horror and disgust when a party partner pulls out a rig.

"Hey, man, what the fuck is that?"

"It's the best way to do it, dude."

"Maybe you'd better take that action somewhere else. It's not cool."

But the thing is, it was cool. At least that's how I saw it. When I encountered a junkie, I didn't see some sad-sack, tooth-less loser with pallid skin and the inability to get through four hours without a fix. I saw a member of the Fraternal Order of Cool. The world heroin addicts occupied was closed off to me, and I was fascinated by it. There was a dividing line between drugs. Some users of cocaine and speed can get downright schoolmarmish when heroin enters the picture.

"Want to try some of this?"

"What is it?"

"Heroin."

"Get the fuck out. Now."

Heroin, like needles, was cool. Or so I thought in those days. I sensed that dope might be the key that could unlock all the doors that the secrets of art, poetry, and music hid be-hind. Charlie Parker had blown mad, furious harmonies under its sway. Keith Richards, the ultimate rock-and-roll outlaw, churned out thick, massive riffs with its influence. William Burroughs took its directives and conjured up dark, nightmarish worlds that I wanted to explore. The whole of the night-framed hip world grooved to its beat and pulse and created fucking art. Smack was their muse. My heroes had known its allure, felt its embrace, and I wanted what they had.

Despite my fascination and desire to explore the dark world

of the poppy juice, I learned quickly that heroin wasn't an easy score. The pill poppers, speed freaks, and drunks I knew just didn't have access to junk. It wasn't something they used and they didn't have connections to that world. The junkies I knew all possessed some strange moralistic code that prevented them from introducing a novice to the habit.

"Hey, man, let me try some of that," I'd say as casually as I could.

"You ever done this shit before?"

"No. But I've done everything else."

"Sorry, kid. I'm not going to bust your cherry."

"But I can pay. I have cash."

"No."

It was frustrating and a major hassle, but if you look hard enough for anything, and if you're persistent enough, you'll find it. So there I sat in an apartment deep inside the Hollywood wasteland. It was a hot night and the avenues and boulevards were crawling and thick with hustlers and twilight life forms. The room was dark and cool, a refuge from the dusty streets. I was twenty thousand leagues beneath a neon sea. Across from me, sitting like Buddha at a low table littered with bent and blackened spoons, misshapen candles spitting out what little life was left in them, needles, glittering squares of tinfoil, bright scraps of rubber that had once been balloons, ashtrays overflowing with cigarette butts, and half-empty glasses, sat a guy named Top Jimmy. He was one of the coolest dudes I knew, an underground legend. I had met him at the Cathay de Grande where his band, the Rhythm Pigs, played every Monday night. A snaggletoothed, porcine throwback to an earlier era's great, hard-living white bluesmen, his given name was James

Paul Koncek, but he derived his blues handle from a counter-man's gig he had once held at a gritty little Mexican takeout joint called Top Taco over on La Brea across the street from A&M Records, where he handed out free tacos and burritos on the sly to struggling musicians and local down-and-outers.

Now here I was in Jimmy's pad about to take my first taste of heroin. I had conned him and convinced him I was a regular user of the stuff. Not strung out, but well versed in the mysteries of the medicine. I was excited and maybe a little scared, without a clue about what to expect. *This is it,* I thought. *This is your first step into something deep, Bob.* I watched him perform the arcane voodoo ritual of shooting up. I was fascinated as he carefully measured out a dose into a bent spoon like some nineteenth-century backwoods apothecary, added some water, and then cooked it over the flame of one of those sputtering candles on the table. When he determined it was ready, he sucked up the solution into a syringe through a wadded-up piece of wet cotton. I watched him tie off his left arm with a cord, find a ripe and juicy vein, and slide the needle in. He pushed down the plunger. Silence.

Jimmy let the rush wash over him, then focused. "You sure you've done this before?" he asked suspiciously.

"Fuck yeah, man," I lied, a little too eagerly.

"You got a point?" was his next question.

My naïveté showed. I was lost. A point? A point about what?

Before I could answer, Jimmy said, "Here," and took my arm, tied me off, and gave me a shot from his own rig.

This was something. A window opened. A wave flooded in and I felt like I was sinking deeper into the underwater world of Jimmy's pad. Street noises filtered in from a million miles away.

I tamped down a slight flurry of panic and briefly felt nauseous, but that passed as I rode the wave and quickly found my sea legs.

I'd never felt so fucking great in all my life. This stuff was something I definitely needed to explore more deeply. I became part of a little clique of intravenous drug users. It was a small circle. Don Bolles from the Germs; Top Jimmy, of course; and a dealer named Earache. I lived at the La Leyenda Apartments, which rose like a dirty, skewed Spanish Art Deco iceberg from the concrete sea of Whitley Avenue. My habit began to grow from that first taste, although I ignored all the warning signs. Lori left me after one too many fuckups. I didn't really care. My interests were becoming narrowed down to three things: dope, drink, and music.

One day, as I made my daily neighborhood rounds, I ran into Flea—the kid who had flipped my records while I DJ'ed—and his friend Anthony Kiedis. I knew Flea as the bass player from Fear, and I loved that band. I didn't really know Anthony except from seeing him around at the clubs. "What's going on, man?" I asked.

"We're starting a new band," said Flea.

"It's a whole new thing," said Anthony. "Punk and rap all mixed up together. Totally unique and new." They called themselves the Red Hot Chili Peppers and they said they had a gig that night at a place called the Kit-Kat Club.

"You should come see the show, Bob," said Flea.

I was always up for new music, so I went and was knocked out by what I heard. I'd had no idea how good they were. It was mind-boggling. They were right. What they had developed was completely different, a hybrid sound. It was energetic and crazy, and they had charisma. I could see they were onto something.

After the show, I caught up with them. "That was awesome! Where are you guys going now?"

"We need to find a place to stay," said Anthony.

"Yeah, we've been couch surfing," said Flea.

"I got you covered," I told them. "My wife left. I have room. Come stay at my place."

They moved in that night, although I don't know if you could technically call it a move since they arrived with not much more than the clothes on their backs. They had been living as close to homeless as it's possible to be without actually living in an alley. I was a little concerned about how they might react to my drug use and drinking, but I saw right away that they were full-on coke-shooting, up-all-night maniacs. This was a living arrangement that could work, I thought.

They had wildly different personalities. Flea was much more like me in those days. We were both a couple of dedicated music geeks. Anthony was too, but he was definitely his own man. He tended to be thoughtful and deep. Here was a kid who had some confidence, I thought. He saw himself as equal to anybody and everybody alive or dead. That kind of self-esteem is rare. Especially for a twenty-year-old kid. Flea and I didn't possess that kind of self-confidence. I still don't. I tried to understand it. What I think is that both Flea and I had somewhat traumatic childhoods. Anthony didn't come to California until he was about thirteen. Up until then, he lived with his mom and stepdad in a very traditional, normal home. By the time he got out here and started living with his nontraditional, iconoclastic biological father, he had already developed his personality. It was set. It wasn't going to change.

Anthony, as long as I've known him, has never felt the need

to explain himself. He's never cared what anybody thought of him. He knew who he was and if you didn't like it, too bad. It didn't affect him. It works both ways for him. If you cross him, you're dead to him. I've had arguments with him, but he's never felt I've betrayed him, so we've managed to stay cool with each other. But, I swear, I have never met anyone who had a better understanding of who he was than that guy. He's self-contained and doesn't need anyone but himself.

Flea and I were different and bonded over our shared musical heroes. All three of us would constantly spin records in our apartment, but Flea and I would take it to an obsessive level. Not long after they had moved in, Flea and I discovered we both loved bass player Jaco Pastorius.

"Wait! I got a bunch of his albums," I said. I dove for one of my crates and started to pull out some of Pastorius's solo stuff as well as his work with Weather Report. Flea started to paw through my records and came up with Ian Hunter's *All American Alien Boy* album.

"Did you know he played on this?" he asked.

It wasn't long before the floor was littered with record albums and old music magazines I had managed to dig out. We were having a ball listening to the music as we quizzed each other with Jaco Pastorius trivia. It was then that I noticed Anthony had come into the room. He looked at us like we were idiots. His arms were folded and a smirk was on his face. Okay, this deserved an explanation.

"What?" I asked as I threw up my hands.

"Why do you guys do that?" he sneered.

"Do what?" asked Flea.

"This fucking idolatry, man. It's kind of sick, you know?"

"Wait," I said. "You mean to tell me that you've never admired or idolized anyone in your entire life?"

Anthony didn't even take time to think about his answer. "No. Never." He gave a derisive snort and went out to buy cigarettes. But Anthony wasn't immune to the appeal of rock idols. While we all enjoyed the degenerate, trashy, punk rock splendor of life at La Leyenda, he became obsessed with the song "Las Vegas" from Gram Parsons's *Grievous Angel* LP.

*Every time I hit your crystal city*
*I know you're gonna make a wreck out of me.*

With doper's logic, Anthony and I had become convinced that underneath the amphetamine whomp of guitars and the brittle vocal harmonies of the track, Gram was speaking to us directly, advising and watching over us as we took turns shooting up speed in our squalid little pad behind the flimsy door that read 305.

Flea, on the other hand, wasn't nearly as big a fan of the early country-rock sounds as Anthony and I were, preferring instead the punk rock drive of Minor Threat and their song "Straight Edge."

*But I've got better things to do*
*Than sit around and fuck my head*

Flea's obsession with that song and its message should have clued Anthony and me in to what would follow. One afternoon, Flea just spilled it. "I'm moving out," he said.

"Where are you going?" I asked.

"Back home with my mom. It's too much here. The drugs and everything. It's all you guys do," he said as he looked around at the squalor, the empty bottles, the mess. His mind was made up, and there was no need for discussion. He walked out and left Anthony and me there to stare at each other in stunned silence. We decided to get high. It was weird. Flea still hung out with us, and he and Anthony were still focused on the Chili Peppers, but Flea was clean and sober.

Their band was already generating excitement on the club scene, and I spent so much time with them, it was hard for me to not think of myself as part of the group. In the meantime, though, I made sure that I held on to my DJ jobs. Those were perfect gigs for someone like me. In the shape I was in, about the one thing I could do with any sort of skill was play records. Still, I started to form the idea that I could manage the Chili Peppers. In my mind, I was the fifth member of the band. I thought I was more a part of the band than was the drummer, Jack Irons. In retrospect, it may not have been the greatest or most accurate assessment of the situation. Worse, my sights weren't set that high with regard to the Red Hot Chili Peppers. "You guys can be as big as the Cramps . . . or maybe even X!" went one of my managerial pep talks.

Anthony had bigger plans. For six months, he and I booked the band's gigs. I'd go to the shows, hang out backstage, and feel like I was part of something. I was connected to the music in a way that my DJ jobs didn't fulfill. I would constantly feed them ideas about music and introduce them to records by Bob Dylan and Hank Williams. Anthony may have had an innate understanding of show business and image—he was a handsome guy who knew how to be cool—but I knew about songs and songwriting, something neither he nor Flea had mastered yet.

One night, at one of their gigs, I noticed a twitchy, fast-talking guy who instantly reminded me of Paul Shaffer's Artie Fufkin character from *This Is Spinal Tap*. He nosed around the band. I thought, *Who the hell is this guy?* I made a few inquiries and learned his name was Lindy Getz and he had credentials. Solid credentials. Getz had discovered Bachman-Turner Overdrive, the Ohio Players, and countless other big-league bands. Now he had his sights set on Anthony. "I want to manage you boys," he said. My first thought was, *This dude's a fuckin' tool. Why would Anthony even talk to a guy like that?* I may have had some connections to get the band booked in the smaller clubs of L.A., but it was painfully obvious that, compared to someone like Lindy Getz, I lacked even the most basic skills and know-how for managing an act that was, by the week, becoming increasingly popular. I hung around and drank too much and did whatever drugs I could get my hands on. Getz was in as the band's new manager and I was out.

I tried to find a role within the group as a sort of aide-de-camp. Why not? The Clash had Kosmo Vinyl. The Chili Peppers had me. I gave them ideas. I introduced them to Funkadelic's music. Because of my input, there's a cover of Hank Williams's "Why Don't You Love Me" on their first record. The album's closer, "Grand Pappy Du Plenty," was based on my suggestion that they do an avant-garde instrumental. But with Lindy in as manager, my official title was changed to road manager. I didn't like that role at all. It basically meant I was a glorified gofer. If someone in the band needed water, it was my job to see that it arrived, but I was usually too busy chatting up people around the band and partying. I was barely competent as a road manager, and it bugged me that I had been demoted even though, deep down, I knew that the Chili Peppers could do better than someone like me. My actual day-to-day life hadn't really changed. I still hung out with Flea and Anthony, but I still felt diminished.

Anthony partied almost as hard as I did, but he was on his way to rock stardom, so he was forgiven. He was the front man and had the luxury of being a hard-core intravenous drug abuser. Within the band's structure, I was expected to work and get things done. I could barely make sure their equipment got onstage. My poor managerial skills spilled over into our life at La Leyenda. I couldn't even get the rent paid on time.

I stumbled home one night and Anthony confronted me. "We had a visitor today."

"Really? Who came by?"

"Some rep for the building's owner. Says you haven't given him any rent money. Dude, I gave you some dough a few weeks ago."

"Don't worry, man. I'll take care of it," I said.

The money I had—including Anthony's—I had spent on drugs and liquor. I couldn't cover the rent. I did have enough cash on hand to buy some cheap, made-in-China hand tools and a decent dead-bolt lock down at the local Home Depot. It was a temporary fix, and outside of the weekly calls and visits from the landlord, it seemed to work.

"Man, you're supposed to be taking care of this stuff," said Anthony.

"Hey, they can't get in. We're the only ones who have keys. I'll give 'em some money as soon as I can."

Anthony sighed.

It worked for nearly four months—until I came home one day and saw a red "pay or quit" notice tacked to the door.

"Did you see the sign?" asked Anthony, who had wised up and stopped me giving me rent money that he knew would not go to the landlord.

"I'll handle it," I said. The next morning, I woke to the sound of drills and hammers just in time to see a work crew remove the door and walk off with it.

"Okay, now what?" asked Anthony.

I grabbed some old bedsheets and tacked them to the door frame. "There you go," I said. Anthony looked unsure. "What?" I said. "It's not like we have anything anyone would want to steal."

It was obvious the whole road manager thing wouldn't work out when we went on the first tour. To the band's credit, they gave me a shot, but I blew it. Hotel bookings, sound checks, equipment logistics—the tour was in a constant state of chaos because I was drunk and high all the time and not doing my job. I was a stumbling wreck who couldn't get anything done. The band hired a guy named Ben Marks to replace me when we had barely gotten out of Los Angeles.

"Look, Bob," said Anthony. "We're bringing in this guy to be the road manager."

"But I'm the road manager."

"You don't know what you're doing," said Anthony. "We need someone who's professional."

"Well, what am I supposed to do?"

I was demoted to roadie. I didn't do any better in that position. Ever moved equipment? It's hard work and it's boring. After the show, when the band got to party, I was supposed to break down the stage and load the equipment for the next gig. Instead, I'd sneak off to get high or hang out in a bar. I knew it was starting to piss off Anthony.

I was dead weight. By the time we got to New York, I was fired. "Bob, you're not doing anything," said Anthony. "Why should we keep you on the payroll?" I didn't have an answer for that. We were at the same hotel where the Replacements had rooms. *Chili Peppers fired me?* I thought. *Fuck it. I'll just go to work for the Replacements.* I approached Paul Westerberg. He was a great guy, witty, funny—and he liked to drink as much as I did. We got into a serious drinking bout and bitched about life on the road, tours, and hotels. I brought up the subject. "So, you know I'm not with the Chili Peppers crew anymore," I said.

"That's too bad, man," he said. He sensed where I was going with this conversation and cut me off. "It's a real shame . . . but you can't come with us."

He was right. It never would have worked. I was a terrible roadie. I was the worst drunk and drug addict out of that whole crew, and that included the musicians. When Paul Westerberg—a man who could consume absolutely superhuman amounts of alcohol—thinks you're an out-of-control drunk, you'd better believe that you've made an impression.

And so I was cut loose in New York like some sad, drunken hobo. I told myself I didn't really care, but the truth was that I was scared and a little resentful that my friends were on their way to rock music stardom and I wasn't. I felt left behind. Within a year of being with the Chili Peppers, I had gone from band manager to road manager to roadie to fired. It was not a good career trajectory. With some money in my pockets, I drifted around Times Square for a week before I headed to Boston for an aimless seven days. I stayed drunk. Eventually, though, it was time to come home to L.A. I had no idea what waited just around the corner for me.

# A MONSTER COMES TO LIFE

Back home in Los Angeles, after my failure as part of the Chili Peppers crew, I didn't know who I was supposed to be or what I should do. Anthony and I had ditched the La Leyenda with back rent owed. He found new quarters and I stayed where I could, but we were okay with each other. In May of 1984 Flea and Anthony invited me to go along with them to see Van Halen play a three-night run at the San Diego Sports Arena, and I jumped at the chance. For one thing, it was a solid conformation that we were still friends after the debacle of my time on the road with them.

We drove down the 5 freeway from Los Angeles, a long, traffic-choked slog through the city and its outer suburbs that didn't lighten up until we hit the coast and saw the vast shimmer of the Pacific Ocean to our right and the buff-colored hills of Camp Pendleton to our left. I sat in the backseat with a bottle of vodka, a bag of coke, and a couple balloons of heroin. It was a long time to be cooped up in a car, and I was wrecked before we reached Orange County. To amuse myself, I sang. I didn't think Anthony and Flea could hear me, but they interrupted me midchorus.

"What song is that, dude?" Anthony asked.

"It's just a song. It doesn't have a name."

"It's good," said Flea. "And you can actually carry a tune."

It was a nice compliment and it felt good. In the back of my head, I had always thought about being in a band, but a singer? I hadn't really entertained that notion on any kind of serious level—despite the brief stint in the downtown art-noise band a few years earlier. Through Anthony and Flea, I became acquainted with a guy named Pete Weiss. He was a drummer and he could be combative. We were about as different from each other as two guys could possibly be when it came to our dispositions, but in some ways, we were incredibly similar. Headstrong. My old friend Chris Hansen knew him from Los Angeles City College, where they had both attended classes, and now the two of them had cooked up the idea to start a band.

One night, Pete came by the pad and told me, "Chris and I started a group."

"Great," I said. "Chris is a good guitar player."

"You're going to be the singer."

"What? You've never even heard me."

"Chris says you were great in that band you guys used to have. Don't worry about it. The worst that can happen is that you'll fuck up."

I was no stranger to that, so what did I have to lose? Besides, from the time I had posed with my little acoustic guitar and sang "Dang Me," I had secretly wanted to be a rock star. Musicians fascinated me. I spent almost all my time with them, and music had long been my passion, but I had never pursued it with any kind of seriousness. I didn't think I had the right look and knowing so many great musicians personally, it would be devastatingly embarrassing to fail in front of them. But after all the years I'd collected records, read rock magazines, and hung out in clubs, I thought I knew a thing or two about songwriting and stagecraft. Chris was convinced this project would work, based on our brief stint in our "art band." I figured I possessed enough charisma to make a go of it, but I was also pretty sure that even if I bombed as a front man, I'd be switched over to guitar and I could hide behind an amp or turn my back to the audience. That was my Plan B. The second guitar player in the group was the late William "Bill" Stobaugh. Why he was a guitar player was a mystery since Bill could barely tune his instrument. Still, he was a completely weird, crazy, and artistic guy. Bill had an unusual background. He had been born in Bahrain, the son of a man who worked for an American oil company, but grew up in suburban Massachusetts. He had come to Los Angeles to attend school, where he received both bachelor's and master's degrees at CalArts. He was skilled as a filmmaker. Parts of his shot-on-film master's thesis were used in the Disney movie *Tron*. He would eventually make film his career, doing a lot of rock videos, including "Higher Ground" for the Red Hot Chili Peppers. He died in 1996 from complications that followed heart surgery. He was only forty-two. On bass we had a boom operator named Jon Huck and, for good measure, we had a third guitar played by K. K. Barrett, another film-world refugee who worked as an art director.

But back then, we all wanted to be a rock band. The Replacements were our inspiration, but once we started to rehearse, we found we couldn't do anything but be ourselves. We tried to play some cover songs. It was a disaster.

"Hey, man, let's try to play 'American Woman,'" said Chris at our first rehearsal, and launched into the main riff. Pete fell in behind him and the rest of us tried to follow. It was a god-awful racket, and I couldn't remember the lyrics even though I had heard the song forever on classic rock radio.

"Hold up, hold up," said Chris as he called the jam to a halt. "This doesn't work." Everybody took a break to smoke cigarettes and crack open fresh beers.

"You know what sounded okay?" I asked as I poured some vodka into my brew. "When we were just fucking around with those chords before we tried to play an actual song. I think if you guys just start doing that, we can come up with some lyrics. At least it'd be our own thing. And I think we sounded pretty good."

"It can't be any worse than 'American Woman,'" said Chris.

We started to jam and fell straight into a groove. It felt right. We definitely had something. We wrote four songs at that first rehearsal that sprang to life straight out of our riffs and jams. "Yes Yes No" and "Positive Train" were collaborative efforts with the whole band. Jon and Pete came up with something they called "Thelonious Monster" and Jon and I wrote "Life's a Groove." It was a productive first rehearsal. We also discussed what to call ourselves. My thought was to use the name the

F.T.W. Experience—"F.T.W.," of course, standing in for "Fuck the World" and "Experience" tacked on as a nod to the Jimi Hendrix Experience. Pete wanted to name the band after the song he and Jon wrote. Somebody noted, "If we call the band Thelonious Monster, we'll have a theme song like the Monkees did." It made sense, and I had to admit, it was a good name.

We rehearsed like that for four months, nearly every night, rough jams and hooky riffs crystallizing into actual songs. I had connections with the bookers at the various clubs where I DJ'ed, so getting gigs wasn't a problem. Keeping them coherent was. I was usually drunk, high, or a combination of the two for our shows, and I know it bugged Pete. I'd rant from the stage about Reagan or religion or something I had seen in the newspaper earlier in the day as I'd introduce a song. Drunks and addicts almost always think they're being witty and charming when, mostly, they're just obnoxious.

"Fuck Ronald Reagan!" I shouted, while, in my peripheral vision, I could see Pete behind his drum kit roll his eyes and throw up his hands as if to say, "Not again with this shit!"

I wasn't in the mood for his judgments. Not again. I could picture him after the show: "Goddamn it, Bob! Let's just play the songs!" Yeah, well, fuck him. I didn't have to take guff off of a drummer. I launched myself straight over the bass drum and through the cymbals and connected with him. We rolled around on the stage while we traded blows.

"Holy shit, you guys! Knock it off!" Chris yelled. I snapped out of it. "Oh, right. We're at a gig. People paid to hear us." Pete and I broke it up and we played our song. The shows were sloppy and chaotic and always threatened to fall apart at any moment, but they were also very punk rock. Cocaine, heroin, methamphetamine, and lots and lots of alcohol made me act foolish more than once. "You're a fuckin' mess, Forrest," Pete said with barely concealed contempt. He was right. I was—but our audience dug the excitement.

Flea had come to a couple of shows and had a suggestion. "You guys need to make a demo record," he said.

"We need a place to do it, man," I told him.

"No problem. I have the hookup."

He certainly did. He was pals with a guy named Spit Stix who had played drums in Fear when Flea was in that band. Stix worked as a recording engineer at a studio on La Brea, just north of Sunset Boulevard. It was a gray building called Rusk Sound Studios. A rather anonymous-sounding name, but the place was owned by Giorgio Moroder. He had won an Academy Award for his score to the movie *Midnight Express* in 1978 and had never looked back. His work in film and with disco and techno acts was legendary. But because he was in such demand, he was never at Rusk Sound Studios, so Stix let us sneak in at night and record. We were all proud of the results.

"Hey, Bob! Did you hear?" asked Chris one hazy afternoon.

"Huh?" I said as I followed a double rum and Coke with a big line of speed.

"Man, Brett Gurewitz from Bad Religion heard our demo!"
"And?"

"Jesus, Bob, try to focus. He loved it. You know he runs Epitaph Records. He wants to record us."

"A record deal?" I said. "A real record deal?"

"Yes!"

This was impressive. Gurewitz came to meet us one night.

"I'd really like to do a proper album with you guys," he said. "I think Epitaph could really do something with an album." We were all in. It may not have been the best deal in the history of recorded music, but it was the first major step for the Monster. Our deal gave us one hundred hours of studio time. With Brett as producer, we went to Westbeach Recorders in Los Angeles at ten every night, where we'd stay until six in the morning.

"Bob, try to stay sober. We've got work to do!" Chris or Pete would plead. I thought the drugs and the booze had worked well enough to get us to where we were, so why stop now? I may have been completely fucked up, but I showed up on time, contributed to the songs, and laid down my tracks. *Baby . . . You're Bummin' My Life Out in a Supreme Fashion* was released in 1986, and I was unprepared for the response it got. Not many months earlier, we'd decided to start a band. We weren't seasoned songwriters or musicians, but now, with a growing reputation for unpredictability at our live shows and a new, professionally recorded album showcasing our act, the *Los Angeles Times,* the *Herald-Examiner,* and the *New York Times* all hailed the record as a rock-and-roll masterpiece and compared it to the Stones' *Exile on Main Street* and Bob Dylan's *Blonde on Blonde.* What the fuck? How did that happen? It was a complete turnaround. Sixteen months earlier, I was just a failed roadie for the Red Hot Chili Peppers, and now I was being called a genius in major American newspapers. It could have gone to anybody's head, except for one important detail. Other than the fact that we had critical praise, nothing else had changed. I was still an unpaid aide-de-camp for the Red Hot Chili Peppers, which mostly meant that I hung out with them and offered suggestions, moral support, and the occasional critique. They never held my disastrous stint as a paid crew member against me, but they never put me back on the payroll either. I was broke.

I needed a job. Luckily, Jon Huck's girlfriend Sosie Hublitz, who later became my second wife, was an art director in the movie business and she always looked out for us. She helped me get some jobs working as a production assistant. Robby Müller, a cinematographer, also helped us find work. I loaded furniture. I was a set dresser. You could always pick up some work on a rock video or a commercial for toothpaste or floor wax. In Los Angeles, there was always some kind of shoot happening. Jon Huck and Pete Weiss kept doing sound work. K. K. Barrett kept on with his production-design work. We were all wired into that film world. We felt like we were the coolest people in Hollywood. I may have been at the fringe of it all, but that business pays pretty well. I worked on a movie called *The Boss's Wife*. One of the stars was Christopher Plummer. I probably made $10,000 just for moving furniture around. That went really far back then, although it could have gone farther if I didn't spend nearly all of it on heroin and cocaine. But those film jobs allowed me to live and eat and be me, even if "being me" led to employment problems. Keeping any kind of job is difficult when you're in a stupor.

The album didn't help us get better gigs, either. Despite all the critical praise heaped upon *Baby . . . You're Bummin' My Life Out in a Supreme Fashion,* we found ourselves playing the same little clubs we'd been playing. When the record came out to such accolades, I was convinced it would change everything. Instead, nothing happened. We just floundered around. We made a second record, this time for Relativity Records. The company signed us solely on the praise we had gotten from the first. The deal we got wasn't great, but we made enough to buy a van to take on tour. *Next Saturday Afternoon* is Flea's favorite album of ours, and even today, I'm proud of those songs.

I wasn't too worried. I had seen the same thing happen with the Red Hot Chili Peppers, who were my de facto business model. They had made their first record, gigged, and didn't make much money. Then they made the second record and started to get booked in places like the Universal Amphitheatre. I figured we'd record the new album and it would make us popular enough to play places like the Hollywood Palladium. *Next Saturday Afternoon* came out in 1987, and we toured like crazy behind its release. It was grueling.

People think, "Oh, you're on tour! That's great! You get to go places, meet interesting people, and see the country!" You don't get to do any of that. You show up and do a sound check, go to a bar, have some drinks, see a dressing room, get wasted, do a show, and then drive through the night to the next show, where the routine starts again. It's not a "See America" sightseeing jaunt. It's fucking work. And it's brutal, mind-fucking work. K. K. and Jon quit under the strain.

"You can't quit now!" I said.

K. K. said, "Dude, I have a real career back in Los Angeles. Tear-assin' around the country in a van isn't doing me a bit of good."

"Jon? Come on, man. We wrote 'Life's a Groove' together."

"Bob, I can make good money back home. I don't need this bullshit. Sorry, man."

They were right. They had real careers. But Pete and I were full bore and wide open. We were all in. Chris was in just because he was a student then and could arrange his schedule to accommodate the band. It was all good to him. And he wasn't a drunk or a doper. He earned a doctorate in linguistics and another one in architecture. He didn't go out. He didn't party. It was music or school with him. Chris saved his money. He didn't spend one unnecessary dime. He even scrimped with his per diem money. But he managed to pay his way through school and eventually bought a house in France from the dough he made in the band.

We toured *Next Saturday Afternoon,* and I felt like a musical success. My ego was in full bloom. And it was time to go cut a third record. It was 1989. Pete and Chris were still on board and we had picked up Rob Graves to play bass and had Mike Martt and Dix Denney, who covered the vacated guitar posts. John Doe from X produced us. Looking back on it, *Stormy Weather* was a good title. It reflected the vibe, both inside and out. There was pressure with this one. Everyone expected us to have a hit and break nationally. Relativity Records had given us a real budget and we recorded at Existia Music Group, L.A., a real state-of-the-art facility. Welcome, my son, to the machine. I was absolutely as convinced as any drunken, drug-abusing songwriter could be that "Sammy Hagar Weekend," a sincere homage to the life of the teenage hard-rock fan and a shout-out to the embodiment of the working-class rocker, Fontana, California's hometown hero, Sammy Hagar, was destined to be a huge hit.

> 'Cause it's a Sammy Hagar weekend
> It's a big man's day
> We got a Metallica T-shirt

*Got a little tiny baby mustache*
*Got a jacked-up Camaro*
*We're sitting in the parking lot at Anaheim Stadium*
*Drinking beer*
*Smoking some pot*
*Snorting coke*
*And then drive*
*Drive over 55, yeah!*

I had been that kid at the stadium. I knew what it meant to be out on a weekend like that, and I knew there were kids all over the country who knew what it meant too. Pete and I did not see eye to eye on the song at all. He didn't even want it on the record. "That's just a joke song," he sneered. "Save it for your solo record, man."

My contempt for Pete grew. How dare he be so dismissive of my great song?

"This song will be the hit of the record. You watch. You don't know," I slurred back at him.

John Doe, our producer—who had always been a huge inspiration to me as a songwriter—told us, "These songs are fucking amazing! You don't play 'em very well . . . but they're really, really solid." Once I heard that, there was no doubt in my mind that this would be the band's shining moment and our big breakout. Then the record came out.

"Sammy Hagar Weekend" didn't go national. It stayed regional. But it did get people excited. We sold out the Palace in Hollywood. Two thousand people at one shot. We sold out a similarly sized club—the Channel—in Boston. I felt like we had made an impression. "Oh, my God, we're rolling! There's no stopping us!" I'd tell everybody. But, in the end, the record didn't hit the mark I thought it would. It didn't hit the mark anybody thought it would. My management team of Danny Heaps and Nick Wechsler took steps to make the band break. They set up a showcase for record-industry executives at McCabe's Guitar Shop in Santa Monica. It was a tiny, tiny space with a stage not much bigger than a postage stamp, but it had history in that any number of well-respected, big-time musicians had done some very special shows there through the years.

"Now, Bob," Danny said. "We need you to be sharp. Be on point. Be cohesive and . . . don't be fucked up!"

"This is an important gig, Bob," Nick said, chiming in.

I knew it. I could sense it. Here we were, primed for an eight o'clock show in front of forty different record company executives.

We blew it.

We were nervous. I had the brilliant idea to parody U2's recent ZooTV tour, throughout which Bono and the lads commented on celebrity and media through the use of costumes, masks, and multiple large-screen televisions. They played stadiums. We were at McCabe's. The microscopic stage cluttered with small-screen TVs just didn't work. Worse, we were out of synch. Our shows had always been messy, but this one needed to be tight. It wasn't. I showed up stone-cold sober and I couldn't remember the last time I had done that. I tried my absolute best. Pete, who had just about reached the end of the line with me, didn't give a fuck. It was another Thelonious Monster train wreck. Whatever game plan we had before we went onstage didn't amount to anything. Everyone just did what they wanted to do. This was a crucial moment and even I realized that we had reached a point where we couldn't be like this anymore. We needed organization. The poor performance we gave and the tepid response we drew devastated me. I knew we were good and I knew we could do better, but nobody but me seemed to want to put in the effort that night. We crashed and burned.

The bright spot was that Bob Buziak, then the president of RCA Records, was in the audience. He was seen as something of a genius because he had taken a bunch of old rock-and-roll hits and packaged them together as the soundtrack for the movie *Dirty Dancing*. He saw Thelonious Monster play at Raji's, a popular Hollywood club, and he approached me after the show.

"Bob, I love your songs, man," he said as he shook my hand.

"Yeah? Thanks. What other songwriters do you like?" I asked as I tried to figure out if he was a real music fan or just some slick businessman.

"Oh, so many. I'm a huge songwriter fan. Off the top of my head, I guess I'd say I like Tom Petty, Neil Young, Tom Waits . . ."

Well, at least we spoke the same language.

"I'd love to sign you, Bob," he said, but there was a slight hesitation in his voice.

"You'd like to sign me, but . . . ," I said.

"I'm not interested in the band."

I understood his reasons. He definitely didn't want or need the trouble that a bunch of drug addicts would inevitably bring. He was a fan of songwriters. He had signed Lucinda Williams and Michael Penn. He liked things to be simple and easy with as little drama as possible. He offered me a deal and I signed immediately. I didn't even think of the band. My ego told me that I was the rock star, not them. What else was I supposed to do? I had just come off *Stormy Weather* and that was a lot of work. After you write songs like that, you need to rest up and recharge and get your mind right for the next round. The only way I knew how to recharge involved lots and lots of drugs. But now that I was signed to a major label, I was under a microscope. There was a lot of money involved and I was expected to produce. Bob knew I was in no shape to flesh out a complete song, so he hooked me up with other songwriters and musicians in the hope that they might steer me toward that elusive Big Hit Record I seemed unable to write. There were some impressive people I was paired with. Al Kooper, who played with Dylan when he went electric; Pete Anderson, who had brought some dirty and authentic Bakersfield punch to Dwight Yoakam's records; Stan Lynch, from Tom Petty's band the Heartbreakers; Danny "Kootch" Kortchmar, a premier L.A. studio guitarist who had left a mighty footprint on the sound of every Los Angeles–based singer-songwriter from the early seventies. They were supposed to help me, but they shut down all my ideas.

"You can't write a song about heroin, Bob!"

I can't write a song about heroin? They say write what you know, and for the past several years, that had been what I knew best . . . along with alcohol and amphetamines. I was a doper. I was a doper before I started the band. It was who I was, I thought. Did people give Keith Richards shit when he wrote "Dead Flowers"?

Well, if I can't write about heroin, maybe I can write about religion, I thought. Everybody can relate to that, right? The reaction was swift. "You can't use Jesus's name in a song title,

Bob. Are you nuts? People get offended. People who buy re-cords!"

I thought I'd write a love song. I tried to write one with Victoria Williams. I had always had a huge crush on her, but she was married to Peter Case. That pent-up emotion came out in our song. It was darkly beautiful. It was about a girl who com-mitted suicide and the observations of a man who once loved her while he ate cake at her funeral. I played it for RCA . . . and they hated it. My manager Danny Heaps thought I was an idiot to even attempt to write something like that. "What the fuck is wrong with you, Bob?" he yelled at me. "You write a song about a girl who kills herself and you're eating cake at her funeral? Who the fuck wants to hear something like that?" I started to become resentful. "If all the people I keep getting hooked up with are such great songwriters, why aren't they writing hits for themselves?" I asked.

Maybe I just wasn't paired with the right people. I went out to Nashville to work with country rocker Steve Earle, who had a reputation almost as wild as mine. He was high the whole time I was there and stayed holed up in a bunker he had on his property. He lived in this weird, ramshackle two-story house. It was like the capital of White Trash City, USA. There was a decrepit, aluminum-sided aboveground swimming pool in the backyard and a dug-out bunker area where his wife and kids weren't allowed to go. It was a freaky scene and a huge waste of time. Maybe if I had been left to my own devices, I could have done something. I know I had songs in me.

Worse, I was so in awe of all these people and what they had done in the past that I listened to everything they said, no matter how ridiculous. Al Kooper is a great guy and a talented musician, but by the time I worked with him in 1988, he hadn't written a hit since "This Diamond Ring" for Gary Lewis and the Playboys back in the midsixties. Flea, who was aware of my difficulties, said, "Don't you see, man? You need to be back in that little room and to play with guys in your own band."

He was referencing the little twin bungalows that sat at the southeast corner of Fountain and Gardner in the heart of Hollywood, where I had lived with the band in a pair of ramshackle cottages that first saw life in the 1930s but were now so weathered and had sheltered so many lives through the years that they stood as haggard and rickety as I was. It was a world away from the sterile Hollywood Hills environment that I'd used my record company advance to put myself in.

Fountain and Gardner was a real paradise for me. It was the last place I had felt creative, as we rehearsed in the second house's front bedroom. I wrote "Sammy Hagar Weekend," probably the band's biggest hit, from our album *Stormy Weather,* there. It was creative and vibrant and cheap. The band members had paid $100 a month for the rehearsal space and I paid $215 for my rent. Keith Morris, front man of Black Flag and the Circle Jerks, had converted the garage of the other bungalow and called that home. It was a chaotic scene, but I could work there. The place was always packed with local musicians and people visiting from out of town. In the back, we had a garden with a patio just made for drinking. Billy Zoom, the splayed-legged, Gretsch-slinging guitarist from the band X, had earlier purchased a brand-new bread truck with his bandmates and then had gotten down to the serious business of converting the inside of the hulking machine to a rolling hideaway. When he finished his project, the results were outstanding. It had heat, comfortable couches, a television, and an upper loft area for sleeping. He was a craftsman, and when X had gotten tired of their machine, Thelonious Monster bought it and parked it in the garden just to have another area in which to relax and enjoy this little private world we had created.

It was like being in a constantly shifting kaleidoscope of faces, some that were well-known on the scene and others, like those of the groupie girls, that were more anonymous. It didn't matter because everyone was always welcome. The guys from the Sunset Strip metal band Ratt would drop by, and their hulking guitarist Robbin Crosby would stay with us for days. Alterna-funksters Fishbone were regulars too, as were the guys from the Red Hot Chili Peppers. Hillel Slovak was always lurking around somewhere, as was his posthumous replacement, John Frusciante, who played with the Monster for a while.

I spent eighteen frenetic, fulfilling, and productive months in that little self-contained world, where I wrote, played music, and just did whatever the hell I wanted to do, whenever I wanted. And those times when we got wasted on the patio and passed around an old acoustic guitar allowed me to make up the songs that eventually led to a bidding war between RCA and Capitol to sign the band. "Leave me alone, leave me alone," I wrote. "Leave me alone in my own backyard. I don't need to be Bob Dylan, I'm Bob Dylan in my own backyard."

"Those are the same chords you used for 'Sammy Hagar Weekend,'" man," said John Frusciante when I played it for him. It didn't matter. I was having a ball and so was everyone around me. Anything was possible there. I would come home some nights to find Karl Mueller, the bass player for Soul Asylum, in my bed in the living room entertaining some girl he had just met, so I'd shuffle to the den, only to find Robbin Crosby shooting speedballs in there. Oh well. There was nothing left to do but go back downstairs and out to the patio and get into whatever might be happening out there, or go next door and watch television with Keith Morris. I was never one to play the heavy and kick people out. Besides, I discovered fairly quickly that being buzzed at two thirty in the morning in a crazy environment was the perfect thing for writing down some useful material. That never happened in that whole dismal year at RCA. It was doomed from the start. I was not wired to work like that. With a band, songs come together organically, naturally. I started to believe that songs like "Sammy Hagar Weekend" were flukes. I didn't think I could write like that anymore.

The drugs and alcohol didn't help. It became obvious that with each week that passed, I cared less and less about writing good songs. I was too caught up in doing drugs and playing the part of a big shot. I was insufferable. And yet, I had the notion that the one thing I loved and the one thing in which I took pride—my songwriting—was being destroyed by my use of drugs. Writing was something that I cared about and here I was tossing it away.

Danny and Nick, my managers, begged me to record just one good song. It could even be a cover song, but all the others would have to be written or cowritten by me so I could get the publishing rights. If I had just been able to take songs from everybody and do those, I might have been able to make a decent album. After a year of this, RCA gave up on my ever writing a big hit. But Bob Buziak still had faith in me. "We can sell Bob," he'd say. "He's an interesting character. He's got dreadlocks.

Let's put him in an Armani suit and pick covers for him to do."
There was the idea to have me possibly contribute something
for a movie soundtrack, and RCA decided that I would sing
Jimmy Ruffin's 1966 Motown hit "What Becomes of the Bro-
kenhearted." Anthony Kiedis rapped over the outro. As soon as
they brought in the female backup singers, I left the studio and
went home. "If this song gets the plays we think it will, it'll be
huge. It can be the lead track on the album!" said the executives
at RCA. The song was never released. I still don't even know
which movie they planned to ruin with this poorly conceived
attempt to manufacture a hit. This felt like the lowest I could
go. A few years earlier, major American newspapers had said I
was Bob Dylan. Now I was Greg Brady from *The Brady Bunch,*
singing somebody else's song and wearing somebody else's suit.
It was just like the episode where record-industry slicksters
with blow-dried hair and polyester shirts tried to shape him
into a teen-pop star named Johnny Bravo. Was this what I had
become?

Flea and Anthony and almost everyone else I knew pointed
me toward rehab. "You have to go, man," they said. "Look at
yourself." The thought terrified me. My identity was wrapped
up in being wasted. It was who I was. It was what made me
uniquely me. "Fuck you guys! You're supposed to be my friends.
You should be supportive! I never said shit when you guys were
slamming dope."

"Because we were addicts, Bob. Now it's just you."

Those words stung. True, we had all been addicts, but Flea
had cleaned up right after we had all moved into La Leyenda.
Anthony had stuck with it longer, but he had managed to kick
his habits recently. They hit even harder when, alone at night,

I listened to those demos I had recorded for RCA. I couldn't escape the horrifying fact that drugs and booze were ruining whatever skills I had as a songwriter. Worse, I had started to not care. I liked to pretend I was still having fun and that drugs somehow made me cool. Weren't all rock stars supposed to be wasted? That my friends couldn't handle the lifestyle just showed how much stronger I was than them. That's what drugs do sometimes. They can convince a man that wrong is right and right is wrong. When he wakes up in the morning and is dope-sick and miserable, he doesn't say, "This stuff is killing me." No, he bangs up a shot, and as the sickness eases he tells himself that he's never felt better in his life. Suddenly, he's Superman.

And then I got the phone call. Professionally, I may have felt fucked up, but on the surface, everything else was seemingly great. I had a cool pad in Mount Washington just north of downtown. I slept a sound, dreamless sleep in the custom-made bed Christian Brando, Marlon's kid, had built just for me. A preternaturally sexy Playboy model shared the mattress with me. It was almost perfect. Or at least it was until six o'clock that morning, when the phone on the nightstand let out a shriek and I bolted upright. The sun had yet to break the horizon but it was close enough to fill the room with that weird blue glow that isn't day and isn't night. The phone screamed again and Ms. Playboy let out an annoyed little moan and burrowed deeper under the covers. I grabbed the receiver. A call at this hour is never good. "Hello?" I said. It was more of a question than a greeting.

"Hey, Bob! What's up?" said a cheery voice on the other end.

The voice was familiar, but my sleep-fogged brain couldn't quite place it. "Who is this?" I asked.

"It's me, man. Al Kooper. Have you heard the news?"

Oh, God. Somebody's died, I thought. I hesitated. Did I really want to know? "No, dude. I've been asleep. It's six o'clock in the fucking morning here."

"Your boy got fired, man," said Al.

"Huh?"

"Buziak's out. Gone. Big investigation or something over there."

"What the fuck does that even mean, Al?" I asked.

"It means you better figure out something fast," Al replied. I said good-bye.

It was too early to call Bob at RCA, so I killed time as best I could. I drank coffee and smoked cigarettes and watched CNN, but the time still dragged. At nine o'clock, I called his office. The receptionist put me through right away. He picked up. "Are you okay?" were the first words out of my mouth.

"Yeah. I'm fine, but I guess you heard. I'm not going to be overseeing your record anymore. In fact, I'm not going to be around to protect you anymore. The drugs, Bob. The inability to write a hit. People around here don't have confidence in you. You should probably call Danny and Nick right away," he said.

"They can wait," I said. "How are you?" I asked.

"Bob, when guys like me get fired, we get lots and lots of money. I'm fine. You need to call Danny and Nick now," he said again.

"Hey, I don't care if RCA drops me," I said. "I have a firm three-album deal. They'll owe me a lot of money if they do that."

"Call Danny and Nick," he said one more time. Click.

I can't say I was surprised when RCA dropped me. I got

some buyout money. What else was there to do but get the band together? I spent the money I had gotten from the buyout to purchase everyone new equipment and to make them feel comfortable with me again after I had left them high and dry when I signed with RCA. Thanks to the competitive nature of the music business, we got a deal with Capitol pretty quickly. They said all the right things: "You know why it didn't work with RCA? That company doesn't *get* you, man! You're a *rock band*. RCA tried to make you into something you aren't. We know how to do this. The budget will be tight, but you'll be in a band again and you'll be on the road three hundred nights a year and we'll make sure you get on college radio."

We signed and recorded *Beautiful Mess*. Of course, Capitol wanted a hit too, and that record didn't have one single on it. Oh, it had some fine music and a lot of great guests, but no singles. And then came the never-ending bus tours. Eighty-nine shows in ninety-three days, two weeks off, and then start the whole thing over again. I'd hide in my hotel room and do drugs.

"Hey, where's Bob? We need to hit the road!"

"He's holed up in his room. Says he's not coming out."

"What? What the fuck's wrong with that guy?"

"Says someone needs to call the label. He wants a bigger per diem. Says he won't come out otherwise. Wants money now."

I could hear an angry fist pound at the door. "Goddamn it, Bob! Let's go!"

Something had to give, and I suspected that it would be me. It was 1992 and a trip to rehab was in my immediate future. I had been down that road before.

# HAZELDEN

*They always say that nuthin's perfect . . . Trust
me, I'm well aware of that.*

**—"Nuthin's Perfect," Thelonious Monster**

I n late January of 1989, under the low lights of a fancy
Hollywood restaurant called Citrus, I sat with people I
trusted and listened to their concerns. It wasn't an in-
tervention. At least it wasn't in the traditional sense of how
you might think of it. Everyone sitting at the table knew me
well enough to realize that any ham-handed attempt to scare
me sober wouldn't work.

"You gotta do it, man. You need to straighten yourself out,"
said Anthony, who had himself recently taken the cure.

"Anthony's right," said my girlfriend Marin.

Danny and Nick, businessmen to the bitter end, just asked me how my songwriting was going. I didn't have a good answer to that. It wasn't going at all. I played with my food while everybody else ate and talked at me. By the end of the meal, I felt like I really didn't have a choice. I agreed to go to treatment. Time to lose my cherry. *All drug addicts go through rehab, Bob,* I told myself.

I knew I did a lot of drugs, but was I really as bad as they all seemed to think? By any measure, for a young guy, I did all right. I lived in a house in the Hollywood Hills, I had money in the bank, and I ate at the Musso and Frank Grill every day for breakfast. They knew me there. "Right this way, sir!" the ancient waiter in the red vest would say as he led me to one of the plush booths. "Shall I bring you the usual?"

"Yes," I'd say, and add, "But yesterday the bacon wasn't cooked enough. Can you make sure it's right today?"

"Absolutely, sir! May I get you something from the bar?"

"Vodka and orange juice, man."

"Excellent choice as always, sir!" he'd say, and smartly march to the bar and quickly return with my order in a tall, cold glass. And there I would sit, sipping my drink until the food arrived. My order was always the same: a couple of the joint's famous flannel cakes—thin, golden pancakes of an uncommonly large diameter, topped with fresh creamery butter and genuine maple syrup—accompanied by a pillow of fluffy scrambled eggs the color of lemons accented with a sprig of fresh dill and a couple slices of crisp bacon.

I lived a sweet life. How many people could say that? But the more my friends talked, the more I became convinced I had a problem. I may have been an alcoholic and a drug addict, but it was still hard for me to really believe it. I thought I had solid control over my habits. When I was at home with Marin, I only smoked heroin. It was my little concession to the domestic life. How many hard-core junkies could stay off the needle like that?

"Please, Bob, just go," Marin said. It made sense. She came from Hollywood royalty: her dad was actor Dennis Hopper, and her mother was actress Brooke Hayward. Her grand-mother was Margaret Sullavan. Her mother's great-grandfather was Monroe Hayward, a former United States senator from Nebraska. Marin grew up on the East Coast and attended prep schools with the Fonda kids. She had gone to Ivy League Brown University. Life with me was something she wasn't exactly pre-pared for.

They wore me down. By the time the check arrived, I had agreed to go to rehab. Two days later, on February 2, 1989, I found myself at LAX and wondered if I had made a mistake. *I've had better mornings, for fucking sure,* I thought. It was one of those shatteringly clear Southern California winter mornings that happen when the dry Santa Anas—the hot, seasonal winds that blow in from the desert—scrub the skies clean and all the happy, normal people of Los Angeles give hosannas and praises in thanks that they don't live in some barren, ice-bound part of the country. They walked around with a particular look on their faces, a frozen rictus that seems to barely disguise an inner scream. Or maybe they really are happy. It's always hard to gauge people here in L.A. It's plastic and fantastic, just like you've heard. At the moment, I hated the sunshine and the blank-faced happiness it inspired, and it filled me with disgust.

I was on a Northwest Airlines flight bound for the heart of

the snowy Midwest. I was a little bit dope-sick and a whole lot hungover. I made my way to the center of business class and found my seat. I wanted to bolt as soon as I sat down. I fought the overwhelming urge to run back to the gate and catch the first taxi home. I'm not a good flier. I'm not a good passenger. I don't like to wear my seat belt. I don't like to keep my tray in its upright and locked position, and I don't like to stow my gear in the overhead bin. The whole machine of air travel is made of rules and regulations and even under the best of circumstances, I have difficulty with it. There was one thing about air travel that I did like, though, and that was vodka and orange juice. I needed mine right now.

I tried to hold it together while the pretty, plasticized attendant gave her practiced rundown of what we were supposed to do in the event of an emergency. Whether over land or water, it didn't seem to me to matter. If something happened, we all knew we were completely fucked. Going down might have been the kindest nudge that fate could have given this bird. The whole thing was out of my hands anyway. No sense in being gloomy and doom-struck. I just wanted my drink.

Before I left for the airport, I had stood alone in the bathroom in front of the mirror and smoked a generous quantity of black-tar heroin. I put a blob of the dark, sticky resin onto a piece of creased foil and held a disposable Bic lighter under it to slightly melt the dose. With a McDonald's plastic straw clenched between my teeth and a flame under the foil, I caught the thick, almost oily smoke that slowly boiled up along the crease like a pyroclastic flow in reverse and pulled it deep into my lungs. I was well rehearsed in the technique and never wasted any of my stash. Even now, with my shaking hands and distracted mind, I could have pulled it off while wearing a blindfold. There were a lot of unknowns in my immediate future, but this wasn't one of them. I knew exactly what came next, the warm embrace of an old chemical friend and a sense that everything would be just fine. Of course, I was on dope, so, really, what the fuck did I know?

I watched my reflection in the cold depth of the mirror and saw my pupils contract to pinpoints while a rush hit me deep down in the viscera and spread to the outskirts of Forrest County, USA. The mirror bit was a little ritual I had. It allowed me to see what happened to me. It assured me that the stuff was working. In a nod to choreographer Bob Fosse and the movie *All That Jazz,* I fanned the fingers of both hands in front of my face and whispered, "Showtime!" at the gaunt and chalky visage in the mirror.

My adventure had begun.

I sat in my seat aboard the Northwest 737 and I could feel my anxiety start to build. When would this peppy attendant stop with the flight safety rundown and get on to the important things, like serving me my booze? She droned on and I sensed movement as the plane taxied down the runway. There was a brief pause before the hum of the engines turned into a banshee's feral howl and the awesome force generated by those screaming turbines pressed me back into my seat like I was a piece of putty. Good. Maybe I could just disappear. I felt conspicuous in the foam recess of my little nest. Something inside of me churned and bubbled and it was a bad feeling.

That was forgotten when I heard the announcement, "Your attendant will now take your drink orders." Relief was just an order away. When the attendant stopped next to my row, I put

on my best face and worked the charm angle: "Two double vod-
kas with orange juice, please!" It was important to keep up my
vitamin C intake. It was also important to keep up my hustle.
Dreadlocked musicians like me weren't seen as rock stars by
the general public back then. We were freaks, and freaks were
dangerous and under scrutiny. The attendant was a lovely young
woman. She looked almost military in her uniform, but she was
nice. She had a sense of humor and exhibited the kind of mercy
usually possessed only by those who nursed the terminally ill.
"We'll just pretend one of those drinks is for whoever is sitting
here," she said, nodding toward the empty seat beside me. I
liked her. So this is what they meant by "the friendly skies."

"We'll serve them one at a time," she joked.

"Make sure you remember me," I shot back as she gave me
my plastic cup filled with ice, my orange juice, and four tiny
bottles of airline vodka. I declined her offer of free peanuts.

I don't think I ever enjoyed a drink so much. The cold bite
of the ice that rattled hollowly in the plastic cup, the sweet tang
of the orange juice, and the tasteless after-burn of the vodka
was beautiful. As the mixture absorbed the surrounding light
it took on the appearance of some strange, unnamed gem. As
I drank, I could feel myself stutter-start to rough, shambling
life. The medicine was doing its work, I thought, and I felt my
strength and confidence return as I leaned back and made myself comfortable. Now I was starting to feel good. I felt even
better when I finished my second double . . . and I ordered
two more.

I mean, seriously, what the fuck was I doing here? My mind
snapped back to the present. I was on my way to Hazelden, a re-

habilitation center planted squarely in a bucolic and serene setting in the generic-sounding town of Center City, Minnesota,
where alcoholics, pill heads, junkies, blow monkeys, and every
other type of drug funneler, drinker, miscreant, and fuckup
known to man or beast could start that long, unsteady walk
toward sobriety and what I had been told was a better life. I
wasn't half convinced. I felt I had been conned. Now, up here in
the clear blue sky, above the clouds, it all seemed like such a ridiculous situation. I was on a two-and-a-half-hour flight by myself, so it gave me some time to think, but I really only needed
five minutes to formulate my plan: Forget Hazelden, forget
rehab, and forget any half-assed reformation. I would connect
at the airport in Minnesota and go on to New York City. Sure,
everyone I knew would be mad at me, but it was my life and no
one pressured me into anything I didn't want to do or didn't
believe in. This whole flight had been a mistake and I needed to
move forward. I'd go to New York, where things were cool and
where I could be myself and avoid people who wanted to hassle
me about how I chose to live my life. They'd get over it.

I was still working out my plan when the plane swooped out
of the sky and touched down in Saint Paul. All airports are the
same: You leave the placental safety of the plane and get squeezed
out into an explosion of sound, light, and shiny surfaces. I felt
like my feet were moving through heavy syrup. I really needed
to find a connecting flight and get to New York . . . *now.*

But as I craned my neck and ran down my options, out of
place in this Midwest bustle where people said "Excuse me"
and "Pardon me, sir," I saw an odd little gnome of an old dude
who was holding up a sign that read BOB FORREST. I had so much

on my mind that it took me a second to realize that he was there for me. He was such an unusual sight, standing there in his shirtsleeves and suspenders when outside the cocoon of the terminal it was well below freezing. He intrigued me. I walked up and introduced myself. "Hi. I'm Bob."

"Are you ready to begin the greatest adventure of your life, young man?" he said through a completely sincere and friendly grin. Had I just stepped into a cartoon? I felt like I was on acid.

I thought to myself, *What the fuck* is *this?* but I had to admit, I felt comfortable around this little guy and walked out with him to the official Hazelden patient delivery mobile in the parking lot. It was absolutely nondescript, like something an undercover cop would drive. I got in and the little guy, Sonny, was a ball of positive energy. He had done this enough that he knew the minds of the clients almost better than they knew them themselves.

"So, before you saw me, you were planning to run, weren't you?"

"New York," I answered. "I was going to go to New York."

"You need money to be bad," he told me.

We drove on through the countryside for a number of silent, wintry miles. It was peaceful. I enjoyed studying Sonny and his calm demeanor. He was a unique specimen. We drove through a gate at the edge of the property and I felt like I had been delivered to a college campus. Hazelden was far from the type of grimy prison my worst nightmares had conjured. It was pleasant and nonthreatening, even though I still had no idea what to expect. Sonny parked and brought me to the detox unit, which was also the check-in area. They were expecting me. I took one look around and thought, *This is how things are supposed to be done.*

Presentation is everything, and the spotlessly clean lobby and my orderly room put me at ease. There were a nurse and a doctor who were friendly, kind, and professional. They knew what they were doing. They took my vitals, checked me out, and got my medical history.

"Surgeries?" asked the nurse.

"I lost part of my finger," I said, and held up the stump so she could see. I had been on a bike when I was eight years old and a parked car's door suddenly opened. I slammed into it at thirty miles per hour and my finger was caught in the hand brake. It was damaged beyond repair, never to return. She winced when she saw it.

"History of mental illness?" she read off the sheet attached to her clipboard.

"Is drug addiction a mental illness?" I joked. She smiled. *At least they've got a sense of humor around here,* I thought.

"Any allergies to medication?" the nurse asked.

"Not so far," I answered. She gave me a quizzical look. "No," I said, clarifying.

"Okay, then. We're ready to get started," she said, and stood to leave. "A nurse will be in shortly. Just sit tight."

I had barely shifted in my chair when another nurse brought in some medications. "Bob, this is Librium. It will help with any alcohol withdrawals you may experience." I swallowed the pill with some water she handed me.

She had a another pill. "Now, this one is chloral hydrate," she said. "It will help a little with the heroin withdrawal." I swallowed that one too.

Finally, she handed me something I recognized. "This," she said, "is Valium. It'll just keep you calm. You may experience some agitation and this will help with that." I could feel the Valium kicking in and I was taken to my room, where I went to bed. Someone on staff came in and monitored me at regular intervals.

I stayed there for the next three days and alternated between periods of chills and hot sweats. I didn't sleep much, but the Valium helped a little. Mainly, I just let my body and mind adjust to this new state of existence. Toxins, bit by bit, left my system, and though I'd definitely felt better, I'd also felt a lot worse. And it wasn't like I was confined to my bed. I was free to get up and go outside, but it was winter in the upper Midwest. That meant cold. The kind of cold somebody from Southern California never gets used to. It meant that when you did venture out, you did it in increments of five or ten minutes before you made a quick scuttle back inside where it was warm. It was on these journeys into the world that I started to meet the other patients who had already completed their detox periods. I could see that, at twenty-eight, I was one of the youngest clients. I thought to myself, *You have to know you have a problem before you start to do nothing about it.* And, yet, here I was, doing something about mine. I felt good about that.

Those three days passed as quickly as any other physically unpleasant event might run its course, and when they were over and I was sufficiently detoxed, I was moved to the rehab unit. I felt sure that the worst of my process was over and I was filled with a sort of cocky bravado that came from my belief that everybody on the staff knew exactly what to do and knew explicitly what worked for people like me. It was simple, really. The staff and the program were designed to instill the clients with confidence and a sense of security that I don't think is available through programs you find these days. This second stage was also where I was supposed to learn strategies to stay off alcohol and drugs. Here, in a controlled environment, it would be easy, but back home it might be different. And difficult. It didn't really matter because I didn't want to get too far ahead of myself.

The unit was set up military style. There were three of us to a room. Here I was, a young rocker, housed with middle-aged professional men. They immediately made me feel welcomed and they were a friendly crew. There was John, a high-powered Chicago attorney who had checked in after badly blowing one of his cases thanks to a long-term cocaine-and-booze habit. Moon was a back-slapping good-ol'-boy airline pilot whose binge drinking threatened to rob him of his livelihood. And, of course, there I was with my dreadlocks. John was the head of our unit and assigned us various homemaking tasks. I was shown my bed before we all went off, single-file, to the cafeteria for a lecture about addiction.

There, in the lunchroom, like a punch in the guts, it slammed me. Maybe it was because I had been in such a fog during my initial detox that I just didn't notice it. Certainly, it hadn't been mentioned in the Hazelden brochures and nobody had brought it up since I had arrived, but there on the wall were the sacred "twelve steps," and one word in particular stood out—*God*. I thought to myself, *There is no fucking way . . .* All of a sudden the tone in my head shifted and I felt like I had walked myself straight into the nest of some creepy mind-control cult. I thought of Jonestown and how a domineering, crazed reverend convinced more than nine hundred of his followers to drink cyanide-spiked purple-drink in an act of mass suicide. *That's what religion will get you,* I thought. It didn't help when I turned my head and saw another poster with the Ten Commandments rewritten and translated into recovery-speak. I was an atheist. My mom was, at best, an agnostic. This was alien territory for me. "You've got to be kidding me," I muttered under my breath. The lecture ended with a period of meditation, which, to me, was just another word for prayer. I meditated, all right. I meditated about how I had paid $14,000 up front to take part in the rituals of organized superstition. I was completely switched off. I had to get out.

Now, this is how the mind of an addict and alcoholic works: It jumps to hasty conclusions. At lunch, convinced that I was trapped in the middle of nowhere with a bunch of religious freaks, I found a phone and called for a car. I went back to the unit and started to pack. John saw me and asked me what I was doing.

"I'm leaving," I said.

"What are you talking about? You just got here," he said with surprise.

"I'm leaving," I repeated. "I don't belong here with . . . *you people.*"

"Hey, man, everything's cool," John answered.

"No," I shot back, "everything is *not* cool! This is some dogmatic bullshit right here!"

"Could you maybe be a little more specific?" John asked without guile.

"All that God stuff," I said. "I can't do it. I'm not religious."

John started laughing. It wasn't a mocking laugh. It wasn't cruel. It was a big, friendly laugh. He was genuinely amused by my outburst. "Bob, *all* these programs are like that. Just don't do the God stuff. I don't. Neither does Moon."

"What am I supposed to do?" I asked.

"You can try the first step and just admit you don't have any control over the drugs and the booze. I mean, is making something happen worth putting in at least a little effort?"

I guessed it was and I took the leap and took the first step. I admitted that I had no control over the pills, potions, and powders. God didn't enter into the equation. It was just me and the bottle . . . and I could never stay away from it for long.

John also suggested I try the fourth step and "take a searching and fearless moral inventory" of myself. I hated the language in which it was put, but I liked the idea. I didn't need God to do that either, although the rigors of that particular step absolutely terrified me. I was twenty-eight, a full-grown man with a career and a name, but I feared the things I might find.

# SUPER-SECRET SOCIETIES

C hange was around every corner when I finished my stay at Hazelden. "Bob, you're going to want to stay in what's called a sober house when you get back home or you won't make it," they told me, but I was hardheaded. "Fuck that," I said. "I have my own house!"

I left Hazelden the same way I had come in—piled into a staff car driven by gnomish little Sonny. He was just as positive as he had been when he had picked me up upon my arrival. "Well, you look like a whole new person!" he said, chuckling. I wasn't so sure about his assessment, but the ride to the airport lacked the dope-sick anxiety I had felt when we made the drive to the facility thirty days earlier. Now there was just a general nervousness. I stayed quiet while Sonny chattered and occupied myself with the scenery that flashed past the window of the car.

My head was filled with questions. For the first time since I was a kid, I was sober. Could I keep it going? Could I be in the air for hours and not drink? What about when I got back to L.A.? What if I slipped into old habits? I didn't have the answers to any of it, and this worry didn't help matters, so I tried to shut it out. "Whatever happens, happens," I told myself. When we reached the airport, Sonny walked me to the gate. He may have sensed my uncertainty because as I left to board my flight he clapped a friendly hand on my shoulder and said, "Take it easy, kid." I nodded my agreement and got on the plane that would take me back home. In my seat, I settled back and shut my eyes. Sleep would be the best way to pass the miles. I slipped into Slumber Land before the plane taxied down the runway and I didn't wake up until I felt the bump of the wheels when they touched down in Los Angeles. I grabbed my bag and deplaned, thrilled to be back home. Outside the terminal, I breathed in the smog-scented air and listened to the hum and bustle of heavy airport traffic. This was home—noisy, gritty Los Angeles—and I was glad to be back. I hailed a cab and told the driver, "Get me home as quick as you can!"

I could feel something was different even as the key slid into the lock on the front door. I knew something was up as soon as I stepped inside. The place was . . . empty. Marin had decided to split while I was away. That was a shock, but nothing I couldn't handle. I didn't really care. The house seemed bigger with all of her stuff gone. And there were other changes. One, in particular, that I had noticed before I left town. A lot of people I knew had jumped on the sobriety bandwagon and had ridden it to what they said was a better life. Now that I had stopped the booze and drugs for the moment, I hoped they were right.

It did make staying sober easier, even though most of the time I felt scared and alone. At least I had company.

I had been introduced to the twelve steps at Hazelden and I continued to attend meetings once I was back in Los Angeles. This was a super-secret society that had its own customs, a big book that spelled out its mission, and, at its core, a set of actions that one had to follow to attain enlightenment and freedom from addiction. Of course, from the start I was schooled in the absolute importance of secrecy. This was not stuff for the outside world. It wasn't fodder for gossip. Whoever dared to break the code of silence would be cast out and forever be condemned to wander the wasteland. Or at least that's how it seemed.

I wasn't completely sold on this organization or its program, but everywhere I looked I found friends of mine or old using buddies who were its devotees. A lot of them were in the music business. A couple were close friends. Under the influence of this system, I found that I was a lot closer to Anthony Kiedis than I ever had been when we did drugs together. But something inside didn't feel right. This community had allowed me entry, but I just never felt truly a part of it. The meetings were full of people I couldn't relate to, even my friends, like Anthony. They seemed to be buying into something wholeheartedly and I was much more guarded and suspicious about the whole idea.

Bob Timmins was a guy who specialized in getting help for entertainers, actors, and musicians. Celebrities. In Los Angeles, there was no shortage of those and a lot of them had drug problems. A former addict himself, Timmins had found a niche and he worked it well. When I arrived back home, I heard about a kind of group therapy meeting that was made up of mostly musicians and actors whom Timmins had put together. "You should go, Bob," said Anthony Kiedis. "It might click with you." It was at a recording studio I was well familiar with, and I got myself together and walked over. It was a Wednesday night. I found my way inside. I stopped dead in my tracks when I saw the group members as they sat in a circle on metal folding chairs and smoked cigarettes and drank coffee from flimsy white Styrofoam cups. *Oh . . . my . . . God. What the fuck am I doing here?* I wondered as I looked around. These were the heroes of my youth. These were guys from all my favorite bands growing up.

I sat down as the meeting started. The speakers began sharing the same generalized secret-society-speak I had hoped to get away from. It was the same spiel I heard at every other meeting I had attended. I just tuned it out. As I daydreamed and looked around at their iconic faces, their songs started playing in my head: *"Don't stop belieeeeving!"* *Oh, God,* I thought, *now I'll never get that song out of my head.*

*"I am Iron Man! Duh duh duh duh duh duh."* *Okay,* I thought. *That one's a little better.*

*"Rock of ages . . . Still rollin' . . . Rock 'n' rollin'!"* This was fun. I was glad to have found something productive to do during this charade. Then, just as I began to groove to my mental jukebox, *he* walked in. His presence was enough to zoom me back to attention. He was my idol. In my mind, he was the greatest musical genius of all time. My whole life, up to this point, down to the brand of cigarettes I smoked, was based on *him.* I was in the presence of slender white royalty. When I was a kid I would sing along to his albums. I had posters of him all over my bedroom walls and here he was, in this little recording studio, breathing the same air as me.

"I tried to kill myself a few weeks ago," he stated with matter-of-fact English reserve. "This struggle with drugs had me at my wit's end. I didn't know what else to do but to swallow some pills, wash them down with some wine, and then walk into the sea off Malibu. Rather dramatic, I know."

The room fell silent. Always the consummate showman, he laughed and said that this was all inspired by the 1954 musical version of the movie *A Star Is Born*.

He flashed his famous smile, which was both vulpine and warm. "I felt just like James Mason as Norman Maine, but the water was too cold." He laughed. "And there was no Judy Garland waiting for me when I walked back to shore." While the other members of the group laughed and nodded, I was torn. On the one hand, I thought, *If this guy, with all his success and talent, has that kind of struggle with addiction, there's absolutely no hope for me.* On the other hand, I thought, *A Judy Garland movie? Are you fucking kidding me? That's totally lame.* I stayed and politely listened to everybody's stories, and I went back the next Wednesday night and the Wednesday after that, and it became a habit. It was entertaining, and now that I was staying clean, there wasn't much else to do. I never shared during the meetings. I just listened. Timmins was a big proponent of the idea that celebrities needed to be protected. They couldn't just mingle with ordinary civilians at open-to-all twelve-step meetings. He had created the equivalent of a club's VIP area for recovering addicts and alcoholics. This clan was tight-lipped and stuck together. It was private and invitation-only. And these people needed these meetings. Although I couldn't see the disease in myself, I could sure see it in them. It was obvious that drugs had taken their toll and these artists had all lost something big.

It was clear to see in their shaky hands and nervous tics. The group members were older than I was, so I kind of assumed the role of the new recruit. I made friends with some of them and we'd meet for coffee and superficial talk outside of these meetings, but I could already feel the pull of my old way of life and it seemed inevitable to me that I'd go back to it soon. I was bored with sobriety. The twelve steps may have been ready for me, but I wasn't ready for them. But I liked the exclusivity of the Timmins group.

It was a weakness of mine. I'd always had an attraction to groups and places that were difficult to get into. And if drugs and alcohol were readily available, all the better. Timmins's meetings always reminded me of a drug-free 01 Gallery, or the Zero One, as everyone called it. In 1981, it was the toughest after-hours place in L.A.'s fashionable Melrose District to get past the doormen. For all its hip exclusivity, the price at the Zero One was right. Ten dollars was the cover, and for that, you could drink your fill and do whatever else you wanted. The doors opened at two A.M. and stayed that way until sunrise, weekends only. The catch was that you had to know a trusted regular to cross the threshold. Even then, that was no guarantee that you'd get in. But, if you did, it was all drinking, drugging, and fucking. I had only managed to gain entrance because I worked there. I was a jack-of-all-trades. I walked drinks to the patrons, cleaned up, and sold speed to a chosen few. The place was owned by a hip art dealer named John Pochna who opened the upstairs area of his gallery as a sort of anything-goes haunt for Hollywood celebrities who didn't want to be bothered by civilian gawkers when they felt the need to get loose. The first time I walked through the doors and up the narrow staircase to the second floor, I felt like I had stepped into an update of what I imagined Andy Warhol's Factory had been like: a space dominated by art, the latest music pumped through a first-class sound system, and lots of pretty women. The walls were decorated with works by Robert Williams, a master of chromelike gleam; punk rock godfather Tomata du Plenty; and other Los Angeles artists. This was a late-night crowd, full of punk rockers, ghostly-pale black-clad artists in pointy shoes and shades, and A-list celebrities. It felt special to work there. It was a hidden, cool world that the rank and file didn't know existed. At the bar sat a burly, talkative guy. *Oh, my God,* I thought. *That's John Belushi!* On the bar were huge, fluffy rails of cocaine, and some of the crowd snuffled it up like hogs at a trough.

I idolized Belushi, though I can't really say I hung out with him. Belushi didn't really hang out with anybody. He drank and did his drugs and when he talked, he didn't talk to you so much as he talked at you. "You" being the audience of millions he constantly saw himself before. This little gig of mine was a great way to meet people. It wasn't long before I earned the reputation as "that kid who knows everybody." I liked my new title and it led to some interesting situations. I was good at making introductions. A well-known record-business A & R guy named Mark Williams approached me one night in regard to one of the Zero One's regulars, David Lee Roth. I knew him because he was always at the club.

"Uh, hey, Bob," he said. "I have this couple here from England and they really want to meet David. Do you think you could hook that up?"

"Well, yeah, I think I can. But David likes to be prepped before he meets new people. What can you tell me about them?"

"They play in a band called New Order. You remember Joy Division, right? This is kind of an outgrowth of that."

"Never heard of New Order. Joy Division was so great, I don't think I'd want to hear anything that followed it."

"They're awesome, Bob. They really want to meet David. They're right over there," he said, and pointed to a pasty, nondescript English boy and his dewy girlfriend who stood off to the side. "That's Stephen Morris and her name's Gillian Gilbert."

"Let me go find David," I said. Mark gave the thumbs-up sign to his English friends and I saw the chick bounce on the balls of her feet and clutch her hands to her chest like an overexcited schoolgirl. I searched every corner in the joint and couldn't find David. Someone said, "I think he's in the bathroom," and jerked a finger toward a closed door. "The bathroom" wasn't technically a bathroom, although it did have a sink. It was more of a storage room that housed some cleaning supplies and a mop and bucket. *What the fuck is he doing in there?* I wondered. I knocked. "David? Are you in there?"

"Just a minute, man!" a familiar voice boomed from behind the door before it creaked open an inch. David peered out, looking every inch the rock-and-roll god that he was, if slightly bug-eyed at the moment. "Hey, Bob. Come in, come in," he said, his face cracking into a huge grin. I slid through the door and there was David with the Disco King, a guitarist who had set the dance-music template with his chart-topping band. David Lee Roth might have been the rock star in the Zero One, but the Disco King was the real badass musician in the place. There was a big bag of coke in the room and David and the Disco King were in good spirits. Each wore a sheen of sweat that was, no doubt, the effect of the night's ration of white powder. "Hey, man. There's a couple of English people who want to meet you. They're from that band New Order."

"New Order? I love those guys!" said David effusively.

"They're good," said the Disco King.

"Well, I never heard of them. Let me go get them."

I left the confines of the storage room and went and found Gillian and Stephen where I had left them. They were giddy at the prospect of meeting a flamboyant American rock star. They didn't really make them like David in England, at least not anymore. Of course, they didn't really make anyone like David here in America either. "Okay, it's cool. Follow me," I said.

"Is he nice?" Gillian asked.

"Oh, he's great. He's David Lee Roth. You'll love him."

I shepherded them into the little room. "Bob, shut that door," said David, and I slammed it hard since it didn't fit in the jamb all that well. With five of us crammed in the tight space, there was barely room to turn around. Introductions were made and the small talk started. Everybody loved everybody else. Then David pulled out the magic bag of coke. "Who's in?" he asked. We all were and spent the next hour dipping into it and babbling about anything and everything. The thing with coke-spurred conversations is that even if they're mundane and essentially hollow, they seem, at the time, incredibly deep and profound. Who knows? Maybe it was, but I have my doubts. Other than the Brits' thrill at getting an audience with David Lee Roth, what made up that night's summit topics were likely forgotten the next day. Little meetings like ours, no matter how pleasant and engaging, can't last forever. Despite the fun we all were having, after an hour or so in the tight grip of that little room, with the temperature rising from everybody's coke-elevated body heat, it was time to move on and grab a cold drink.

"Hey, Bob, get the door," said David. "We could all use some fresh air." I gripped the knob to give it a twist and pulled. Nothing. I pulled again. The door was stuck. "Hey, Bob, quit fuckin' around," said David.

"I'm not kidding, man. This door's stuck," I said, and I wiggled the knob and pulled with both hands to emphasize the problem.

The Disco King kept his cool. "This ain't good," he said, but showed no panic as he leaned casually against the wall. The English girl, Gillian, seemed to come down with a sudden case of claustrophobia. She didn't say anything, but her eyes widened like a cat's during a thunderstorm and her breath came in short, sharp gasps. "Oh, my God," she said quietly. Stephen didn't say a word and faced the situation with typical English stoicism. Then David attempted to lighten the mood. "I wonder how much oxygen we have left in here," he said.

Under the influence of cocaine, the conviviality and sparkling wit that can often result from a few well-managed rails is often replaced by raging paranoia and panic once the dose is increased. We had already gone well past any semblance of recreational use in that little room. David's ill-timed reference to an old episode of TV's *The Lucy Show,* the one that had Lucy and Mr. Mooney trapped in a bank vault, was meant as a joke, but people can get a little weird after they recognize that all avenues of escape are closed. They can get downright spooked if they're gakked on coke. There was a crush at the door as everybody but the Disco King tried to claw his or her way out. It was like a small-scale reenactment of the Who's tragic 1979 concert at Riverfront Coliseum in Cincinnati. Compressive asphyxia wasn't even a remote possibility in that little room, but we all wanted out just the same. I gave a holler and hoped somebody on the other side of that door might hear. David ripped out one of his patented stage squeals. The Brits, being more reserved, just banged on the door with flattened palms. The Disco King merely observed the scene with detached amusement. Because the sound system at the Zero One was in maximum overdrive and the guests were caught up in buzzy little worlds of their own, no one heard our pleas. Or, if they did, they just figured it was private business and let it pass. We weren't going anywhere. As that thought sank in, we all relaxed and caught ourselves. Then David said, "Man, I can't believe we're trapped like this." That started another round of staccato raps on the door and screams to be rescued. After about two minutes of this idiot show, someone passed by and heard the ruckus. A good, strong push from the outside sprang the door from the jamb and we all tumbled out, looking sheepish. All except for the Disco King, who just adjusted his blazer and strolled out like a man in complete control of his surroundings. "That was *crazy!*" said David. We scurried off in different directions to our own ends with the understanding that what had happened in that room stayed in that room.

I thought about that code of silence as I sat with the Timmins group. I also could see how the party scene had changed over the course of the eighties. What started out as reckless good times at the beginning of the decade was rapidly devolving into something less fun. There were consequences. Bad press. ODs. Arrests. Tragedies. That kind of thing couldn't be hidden forever in a town like this, although an army of press agents and managers tried its best to keep scandal, dangerous behavior, and dope-addled lunacy out of the public eye. More and more of my old party pals either had checked in, had checked out, or were knee-deep in the process of transformation. The newly reformed were fervent, and groups like the one Timmins ran, as well as other, more egalitarian rehab programs, gave us all a place of shelter and support. And, I had to admit, I thought things looked bright for me. I had a decent contract. My management worked tirelessly for me and it appeared that my music career was on the move. People trusted me again. They had faith in me. Sobriety was like a metamorphosis. But while I could see it happen to the people I came to know in Timmins's circle, I couldn't feel it happening within me. I was just going through the motions. So I went to more meetings and I talked one-on-one with people from all walks of life who supported and encouraged me and held themselves up as examples I could follow. It wasn't like their message was that difficult to understand: Don't get high. All fine and dandy in theory, but I felt like a fraud. When one of my old dope buddies offered me a taste, I didn't hesitate and I found myself right back where I started. I put in eight months of sobriety for that first go-round and, until 1996, fell into a hellish routine of sobriety, another trip to rehab, and, always, the inevitable relapse. I racked up an impressive, if mostly failed, record of attempts to kick the habit. Before it was all over, I'd see twenty-six tries at a cure. But as I felt the dope hit me and I started to nod, all I could think in the crystalline moment was that the drug life was the best and most exclusive secret society of them all. And it was where I belonged.

# VIPER ROOM

I t was junkie bravado. I figured everything was still okay. The money I had seen in '89 was gone, but I had the keys to the Viper Room. The house in Mount Washington was gone, and I couldn't pay the rent at the apartment I kept over on La Brea that I used as a place to arrange drug deals for my friends to ensure the survival of my own ever-increasing habit, but I still went on the road and played concerts. "Everything is okay," I told myself. I couldn't sense it, or maybe I just ignored it, but things weren't as okay as I thought. They were on a steady, inevitable approach to critical mass. I had always loved the records of the old Delta blues singers ever since I first heard them as a kid. Trouble and hard luck were a bluesman's best friends, but I wasn't from Mississippi, and Hollywood in October of 1993 was a long way from the Delta.

I had been catapulted into this strange place once Thelonious Monster's first album hit it big with the critics. It was a place where all things were possible and most things were permissible, an intersection where the worlds of music and film collided and partnerships and friendships were formed. A young actress, known to prime-time America for her work on a popular sitcom, approached me in a club.

"You're Bob Forrest, aren't you?" she asked in a breathy voice.

"That's me," I said. I recognized her right off, but I didn't want to seem starstruck.

"I *love* your band! The last record was great. I dance to it all the time."

I snuffled back my postnasal drip, the result of the coke I had just snorted in the bathroom. "Can I buy you a drink?" I asked.

"I'm leaving. There's a party up in the hills. Do you want to come?"

Of course I wanted to. She was beautiful.

"Here's the address. I'll see you up there." She smiled.

I went and mingled, just like I did in my early days on the rock club scene, and if you're anyplace long enough and often enough, people get to know you. Most of the young actors at that time were deeply into music, and they accepted me. It didn't hurt that they liked my band. It wasn't a superficial thing. They loved music the same way I did. It was passionate and deep. They understood the language. Actors these days might associate with the music scene because they think it's a hip thing to do, but in the nineties, they embraced the cultural revolution the music represented.

Johnny Depp, in particular, had an innate understanding of and love for the Los Angeles music scene. He also had really good taste. I think the only other person who had as much feel for music was Red Hot Chili Peppers guitarist John Frusciante, who lived, breathed, and slept it. Frusciante was what we all considered a true artist. The son of a Florida judge, his passions were his guitar, his music, and his drugs. I think he loved narcotics even more than I did, and he actively promoted them to anyone who'd listen.

I think Depp fit in with us because he had originally been a musician. He was an accomplished guitarist, and I hit it off with him right away. We already had mutual friends, and we formed a tight little group. Johnny and River Phoenix made up the actors' wing, while John Frusciante, the Butthole Surfers' Gibby Haynes, Ministry's Al Jourgensen, and I held down the musician end. Most of us were seriously committed to our poisons of choice and no lectures, warnings, or treatments were going to dissuade us from our off-hours pursuits, which, in those days, involved a lot of coke. We spent a lot of time at John Frusciante's house up in the hills above Hollywood, where Johnny would busy himself filming footage for a planned rock documentary.

"Hey, John," I'd ask Frusciante as we cooked cocaine and baking soda on the stovetop and turned the mix into crack, "do you think it's a good idea to have this stuff filmed?"

"I got nothing to hide," said Frusciante, his unwashed hair falling across his face as he kept an eye on our kitchen chemistry experiment. "When did you get so uptight?"

"I'm not uptight. It just seems that this might be a bad idea."

Frusciante shrugged. "Drugs are never a bad idea," he said

as he carefully dripped cold water into the jelly jar that held the cocaine mixture and started swirling it. The goop inside became a hard, white biscuit almost immediately.

"Dinnertime!" he called out.

We broke off a chunk and shoved it in a pipe. He was right, I reasoned; among this crew, who cared if anyone knew about our habits? Besides, the crack was calling.

River and Johnny, whose looks were their living, had to know when to say no. River—who loved to party—would clean up whenever he had to do a movie. I admired his fortitude. He had the enviable ability to just stop. Johnny mostly kept to the booze and didn't use drugs. But when he was around us, they were always there. I think he was fascinated by it. I don't ever remember Johnny joining in . . . but he liked being there in the middle of it all.

Johnny, flush with money from the Fox network's teeny-bopper cop drama *21 Jump Street* and his rapidly growing film career, along with actor Sal Jenco, had the idea to build a nightclub that would double as their own personal clubhouse. It made sense since Johnny and Sal always thought of themselves as a little self-contained club anyway. That's how they approached the idea. I stopped by one night on my way back from the Whisky. From outside I could hear the knock of a hammer and the high-pitched whine of a tile saw. I knocked on the door and Johnny opened it, wearing a tool belt and knee pads and dressed like a workman. "Hey, Bob! Come in! You really have to see what we're doing here!" He ushered me in and all I could smell was sawdust.

He beamed like a kid on Christmas. He was so proud of this space. Over in the corner, Sal pounded nails. Johnny laid the tile. They would call this spot the Viper Room. Johnny kept up the rundown: "It's going to be great, man! We're going to have bands in here!" Their idea was to create a great nightclub in Los Angeles for their friends. It didn't hurt that Johnny was high profile. When the club opened in 1993, the first band to hit the stage was Tom Petty and the Heartbreakers. The next night, the Pogues played. At that time, neither was what could be called a club band. They played big venues. The Heartbreakers had just done a gig at the Forum in Inglewood. But it seemed that every band wanted to play the Viper Room. It was a prestige gig, and the list of bands that played there was impressive: Oasis. Counting Crows. Joe Strummer. And the place only held about one hundred people.

I even booked some acts there. There was a young folksinger who was getting some buzz. He called himself Beck. Blond and blank eyed, he wasn't much more than a kid. I had heard a demo of a song of his that had the funny title "MTV Makes Me Want to Smoke Crack." I had been given a copy of it when I had been on tour, and I loved it. I couldn't stop playing it. When I got back into town, I saw Johnny. "You gotta have this kid Beck play here. He's great." Johnny, wired into the music scene like always, was aware of him, so we booked him. It was Beck's first important gig in his hometown. He had a prime slot, ten o'clock on a weekend night. L.A.'s music scene at the time was not all that receptive to a solo neo-folk singer, and Beck knew he had to sell himself as something unique. He was also something of a performance artist. He had a crazy gimmick. In addition to his acoustic guitar, he would wear a gas-powered leaf blower on his back, just like the ones every landscaper and maintenance guy from the Hollywood Hills to the Malibu canyons strapped on as they did their magic on the homes and estates of the rich and pampered for whom they sweated and slaved. While a DAT machine played prerecorded music, Beck would dump a trash bag full of dried leaves, twigs, and yard clippings all over the stage; crank up his blower; and scatter-shoot the audience with vegetable debris. It was weird and it was goofy, but it was just the kind of thing that could help a fledgling folkie get some attention in '93.

The night Beck took the stage at the Viper Room, Johnny was out of town. Beck did his act, complete with the leaf blower. Sal was going nuts, and not in a good way. I was watching the show and Sal was practically pop-eyed. "What the fuck is this kid doing, Bob?"

"Sal, he's the guy that sings that song about MTV and crack. He's great, isn't he?"

"Get him the fuck off my stage!"

Poor Beck. The audience was hostile. They booed him. It was a train wreck. Here's this twenty-three-year-old guy on-stage who looks like he's about fourteen but sings in the voice of a seventy-year-old black man from Arkansas . . . all while he blows trash and leaves into the audience. Some people tossed the trash back at him. Others yelled, "You suck!" Sal was livid. I said, "You have to wait until he sings the song about MTV!" Sal told the sound guy to shut down the PA.

"Sal, you're a dick," I said. "I'm telling you, this kid is great."

Sal responded, "That kid ain't fucking shit. And you're not booking things here anymore, Bob."

I went outside after and found a dazed and confused Beck on the sidewalk. "Don't worry about it," I said. "I thought it was a great show . . . but maybe the leaf-blower thing is too much. Just play your songs." Beck was concerned. "Am I still going to get paid?" he asked. He was disappointed, but within the year, he was a local hero. He made the *Mellow Gold* album and you couldn't turn on the radio without hearing him. Now that he had made it, every hipster in town claimed to have been at that show and they all testified how weird, chaotic, and mind-blowing it was. The truth is, there were only thirty-eight people there that night, and they all booed because they didn't understand Beck at all.

Despite that misstep, I remained part of the club's inner circle.

Because everyone had such high profiles in those days, we knew we were being watched and we tried to be careful. The paparazzi were constantly skulking around and the supermarket tabloids paid big bucks for embarrassing photos of young TV and film stars. They didn't seem to care about rock musicians as much. There was constant back-and-forth between Frusciante's place and the Viper Room. His home wasn't more than two minutes away from the club, and we'd all make these mad dashes over there.

"Hey, we're going to Frusciante's," I'd say.

"Aw, man, there's some creep with a camera out front," Johnny might answer.

"Look, just lie down in the backseat. I'll drive. They won't follow me."

I'd grab the keys and pile everyone in the back. Then I'd blast out of park and jet down Sunset.

"Turn right at the next light, Bob!"

I'd spin the wheel.

"Christ, Forrest, I'm getting seasick back here! Take it easy."

"I think someone's following us," I'd say.

"Can you tell what kind of car?"

"I don't know. Maybe a Benz."

"Aw, fuck, Bob. Those photographers all drive crappy cars. Ease up."

It was real cloak-and-dagger stuff, and kind of fun. We all lived close to one another. Johnny only lived a couple minutes' drive from Frusciante's house and the apartment I kept nearby. The Butthole Surfers' Gibby Haynes, when he was in town, mostly stayed with Johnny. Sometimes I'd stay there or at Frusciante's. I was hard to pin down. River usually stayed at St. James's Club on the Strip, a flashy, high-end art-deco luxury hotel, also known variously as the Argyle or the Sunset Tower. The Viper Room was our headquarters, but Frusciante's place saw almost as much use, although things had started to take on a dark and forbidding atmosphere there. It still didn't stop anybody from dropping by. If any of us were working or out on tour, Frusciante's house was the first stop as soon as we arrived back in town.

Frusciante's place offered something the Viper Room had in short supply: privacy. But that also made it a liability. What had started out as a party place had devolved and spiraled into some dank drug den. Walls were covered with graffiti. Furniture was damaged. Walls and doors had huge, gaping holes. There was a current there—bad vibes and degeneracy. It was out of control and the kind of place that could make the hardest of hard-core junkies blanch and run in the opposite direction.

A few days before Halloween, Abby Rude, the wife of actor and writer Dick Rude, was set to celebrate her birthday. Dick had established himself as a punk rock screenwriter and actor through his association with British director Alex Cox and had worked closely with him on movies like *Repo Man* and the spaghetti-Western homage *Straight to Hell.* Abby was also involved in the film industry and worked as River's personal assistant; her duties sometimes required her to prepare his vegetarian meals when on location. Her birthday celebration was held at the Hollywood Athletic Club on Sunset, an old, sprawling Spanish-style complex that had started out in the twenties as a health club but had been used since its construction for everything from housing the University of Judaism to being a very popular billiard parlor. In the mideighties, the property had been acquired by Michael Jackson's family and housed offices, a nightclub with a two-thousand-square-foot dance floor, and one of the best sound systems in town, along with a restaurant and bar. It was a popular place for the Hollywood crowd to have private parties.

When I got there, River was already at the table. I hadn't seen him in at least three months, since he had been in Utah shooting a movie called *Dark Blood,* in which he played a young, doll-making recluse awaiting the apocalypse on a nuclear test site in the desert. He asked me about his friend right away: "How's John doing?"

"Dude, he's getting worse all the time. Constant drugs," I told him. "It's madness up there at his place." Frusciante's house was even getting hard for me to visit. When I wasn't at my apartment, I tended to stay with Johnny Depp. His place had a much more stable feel to it.

River seemed confused by what I'd just told him. He also may have been a little intrigued. "What do you mean?" he asked.

"I stop by nearly every day," I said, "but it's really fucking nuts there. The place is filthy. It's a mess. John and everybody write all over the walls. Do yourself a favor and just stay away."

What I was really trying to put across to him was that he wasn't like the rest of us. I may have been with a strung-out crew, but I felt like musicians were used to that life. Actors were more delicate. River had just had three months of healthy, drug-free living. Just walking in the door of John's place and taking a deep breath might lead to an OD. I felt a little responsible. He didn't seem to get it, so I spelled it out. "Look, man," I said. "You haven't done any drugs for months. You shouldn't go up there. If you want to see him and say hello, he'll be down at the Viper Room later. Trust me, it's past the point of fun up there these days."

Of course, you can never tell anybody what to do if they don't want to listen, and River, being River, went straight from the party to John's house. Forget the plush room he had at St. James's Club. He stayed with John for the next few days and probably didn't get a minute of sleep. The drug routine stayed pretty consistent for all of us. First, smoke crack or shoot coke directly into a vein for that ninety-second, electric brain-bell jangle. Then shoot heroin to get a grip and come down enough to be able to carry on a conversation for a few minutes before you start the cycle again. Just like the instructions on a shampoo bottle: lather, rinse, repeat. Always repeat. These sessions could last for days and would only end when someone fell out or other obligations intruded. And we'd write and record songs (and lose them), which is what River and Frusciante said they were doing, but one look at their hollow eyes told me they'd also been deep into a major-league drug binge.

When I walked into the Viper Room at about seven on

the evening of October 30, the long fall shadows had turned to night, but it seemed like any other evening there. Sal was excited. "Frusciante and River are going to play tonight!" he said. River considered himself a musician. He had busked on the street as a kid and had continued to play guitar through his teens. He was proficient and he liked to jam. A few years earlier, when he had starred with Keanu Reeves—another aspiring musician—in Gus Van Sant's *My Own Private Idaho*, the grim tale of two hustling male prostitutes, River had carved out time for music despite the tight shooting schedule. Flea, who had a cameo role in the movie, stayed with River and Keanu in the rental house they shared on location in Portland, Oregon. A couple of times a week, they'd hold late-night jam sessions, which provided River with his rock-and-roll fix. Back home in Los Angeles, he had formed a band called Aleka's Attic that got attention mainly because he was River Phoenix, which must have frustrated him. Playing with Frusciante, I'm sure, validated him. He was more than just a Hollywood actor who dabbled in alternative rock. Sal was giddy about it. I wasn't so sure. I knew what those two had been up to over the last few days and could just imagine what kind of disaster they'd whip up onstage.

"Dude, you can't let them get up there," I said, now taking on Sal's part from the time I had booked Beck.

"No, no. They recorded a song. They played it for me. It's going to be great. They're just opening for P, anyway," he explained.

P was a band that had come together from everybody hanging out. Gibby, Johnny, and Sal formed the core, and a revolving lineup fleshed them out. That night, Al Jourgensen and Flea were joining in. It was fun to watch some of the biggest rock and movie stars of the time getting together to play original material and lots of covers. They even had a song that mentioned River. It was called "Michael Stipe," a name-check for R.E.M.'s front man. There was a line that went, *"I'm glad I met old Michael Stipe, I didn't get to see his car. Him and River Phoenix were leaving on the road tomorrow."* It promised to be an interesting night, so I left for my apartment on La Brea to arrange a few drug deals and keep myself supplied in the process. Once business was completed, I went back to the Viper Room at about nine. I walked in the door just as River and John finished their set. It was about what I expected. Maybe a little worse. I went back into the office where we usually hung out and needled Sal. "Hey, man, they're so fucked up they can't even get through a song. You can't let 'em get back up there."

River and John stumbled in. There was a crowd coming in and out. River's brother Joaquin—who went by the name Leaf back then—and his sister Rain were both there. They seemed like kids. Joaquin was nineteen, not even old enough to drink, and his sister was twenty-one. Somebody broke out the coke and passed it around. River was obviously wasted and was as unsteady as a boxer who had taken one too many head shots during a fifteen-round bout. His complete lack of motor skills made me suspect he was drunk. Heroin will make users lean when they stand still, but you almost never see them stumble and fall. Coke fiends may have hands that tremble, but the kind of stuporous shuffle River had made me think he was drunk. Sloppy drunk. He wobbled whenever he was on his feet. Frusciante was completely out of his mind. I had seen him like this before, and even though he was a friend, when he was in that kind of state, he could be very unpleasant. It was as if he didn't operate in this dimension at that point. I sat at the desk and wondered if maybe we all shouldn't go into the secret "party" room that Johnny and Sal had built when the club was under construction.

John and River stood up, unsteady, and went out to watch P do their set. I went out with them. They sat on the stage near the front door and watched from there. I hung back and enjoyed the show. They were always a fun band to watch, and tonight, they played well. It was great fun until I felt a hand tap my shoulder and turned to see River. He was a whiter shade of pale. "Bob, I don't feel so good. I think I'm OD'ing."

"What? Are you sure?" That's something no one had ever said to me. Usually you just OD and that's it. "River, you can't just come up to me and say you're OD'ing." He stood there and rocked tentatively off the balls of his feet in a vain attempt to counter gravity. This club was no place for him at the moment.

"C'mon, man. Let's get you home, then," I said, and tried to guide him toward the door.

"I don't know, Bob. I think I'm all right now." Color returned to his face.

I tried to reassure him. "I don't think it's an OD. You can stand and you can talk." He nodded and turned. I still have guilt that I dismissed his worries so casually.

I watched him zigzag back to the stage, where Frusciante still sat. I was dumbstruck. *What the fuck just happened?* I thought. It was a horrible moment. What was I supposed to do? From where I was, I could see him, so I kept an eye on him for any signs of imminent collapse, but he seemed okay. I wasn't a stranger to overdoses. It was something that happened given the dope-fiend lifestyle. A few weeks earlier, at my place, one of the bodyguards for Ministry's Al Jourgensen had collapsed after a night of heavy partying. I called 911 and an ambulance took him to the hospital. Later, after he had been revived and a Filipino orderly wheeled him through the emergency room lobby, where a few of us had waited for him, he said from his wheelchair, "If you guys stole my dope, I'm gonna kill you— and I'm looking at you, Bob Forrest." He knew me too well.

Not long after I spoke to River, there was a sudden commotion in the club. Someone was shouting to call an ambulance. A current of panic shot through the Viper Room. I could feel it. There was a jam-up at the door, so I pushed my way through to the sidewalk. Samantha Mathis, River's actress girlfriend, was screaming. River was seizing on the sidewalk. Flea was on the ground next to him and tried to do what he could to help. When I saw the scene, I stopped in my tracks. "What the fuck is going on?" I thought. It was only about thirty minutes after River had played onstage. Now here he was crumpled on the sidewalk. He was alive, because his arms and legs shook like he was having an epileptic fit. An ambulance wailed to a stop and the EMTs bundled him onto a gurney and quickly got him inside. Flea jumped in and rode with him to the nearby Cedars-Sinai Medical Center, not too far west in the Fairfax District.

I didn't know the full extent of River's condition, but I knew that whichever way things went, it would be trouble. And it would be the kind of trouble that made front-page news in a celebrity-obsessed town like Los Angeles. I could picture one of the tabloid TV shows like *A Current Affair* blasting out a teaser: "River Phoenix overdoses at Johnny Depp's Viper Room. . . . Is Young Hollywood out of control?" This would be bad, it would be terrible, and we were all right in the middle of it. It

1965: My mom loved getting dressed up to go anywhere, and church was as good of a place as any.

How many junkies have a Catholic school picture
just like this one? Thousands? Millions?

High school prom, June 1977. I had not discovered punk rock yet. Rod Stewart rules.

1991: Me and Elijah. I was clean for a minute after one of my twenty-four rehab stints. My only regret is what pain I may have caused Elijah.

High school graduation.

1982 or 1983: In college, but drugs and rock and roll are calling.

I finally made it. Only twenty more rehabs to go.

Thelonious Monster
Beautiful Mess

ON

SIGNAL/CAPITOL

COMPACT DISCS

AND

CASSETTES

Two of the most important people in my life, Elijah Forrest and the mighty Pete Weiss. © GREG ALLEN

This is as close to my bottom as there's a photograph of. © REDFERNS

Dix Denney, me, and Pete. There were moments when we were magical.
© REDFERNS

1995: My last rehab! Cri-Help in North Hollywood, California. It was visiting day, like in prison.

1996: Me, six months clean, and Max in our first apartment ever. We had been wandering for four years from drug house to motel to cars to her parents' house.

1996: Elijah finally gets a dad. He came for the summer and ended up staying for four years. Looking back, I realize I tried too hard to redeem myself with him. I pushed him too hard too fast.

1996: Let the resurrection begin. Working at Millie's Cafe—six days a week, ten hours a day. "How ya feeling today rock star?" was a favorite joke around there. Taught me humility or humiliation. Close enough.

Viva le Joe Strummer! My childhood hero. One of the biggest influences in my life. This was taken just before he died. I cried the day I got that news more than I had ever cried about anything. I cried for a lifetime over his death. © JOSH GUNDLING WILLIAMSON

2010: Las Vegas, Nevada. My little family on our wedding day. Sam, Elvis, and me.

2010: Anthony Kiedis—the leader of our gang! My spiritual adviser. © GETTY IMAGES

Drew Pinsky became the older brother I never had.
© WIREIMAGE

Gibby Haynes and me, two sober dads, 2012. © JASON
KEMPIN/GETTY IMAGES

Elijah, Flea, me, Chad Smith, and Josh Klinghoffer. We've come full circle. Let the healing begin. © GETTY IMAGES

never even crossed my mind that he could die. My emotions were tangled by all this. I felt awful that River had collapsed. I may have been a junkie, but I was human, and I had empathy and concern for my friend. But I was also fearful that the rest of us could be hauled in for questioning.

It took a while for everyone to get it together, and we each handled it differently. Al Jourgensen and his girlfriend Sean Yseult, the bass player for White Zombie and the daughter of an Ernest Hemingway scholar, went back to their hotel room and laid low. Gibby and I decided to go to Cedars and check on River's condition. It was three o'clock on Halloween morning. Hospitals are spooky places to begin with, but the day and the stillness of the hour only compounded the unease. We parked the car close to the entrance so we could make a quick escape if one was needed, and we walked into the sickly, greenish light of the ER. The admitting nurse must have guessed by our clothes and hair that we were somehow connected to River because she asked, "Are you family or friends?"

I said, "Of River's? We're family."

She looked stern and solemn and waved us past. I saw Samantha standing alone. She was crying. I knew just by looking at her that River was dead.

I went numb. It was so unbelievable. Gibby and I were in shock. River partied, for sure, but nothing at the level of the rest of us. *How could he be dead?* I wondered. I wanted to give my condolences to Samantha but realized there was nothing Gibby and I could do here. Our presence might only make things worse. To her we probably represented evil. The press didn't know yet that one of Hollywood's most promising young actors had just overdosed on drugs and died. Gibby and I went back to the car and sat there for a while as we tried to wrap our minds around the situation. The reality of this tragedy hit me like a sudden punch to the gut and I sobbed, "Oh, my God! Oh, my God!"

"This is going to be bad, man," Gibby said.

"What do we do?"

"Where's Frusciante?!?" we both asked.

It hit us like a bomb that John might be running loose. He was the weak link of our group. He was likely to say anything to anyone, even reporters—"We all *love* drugs! They're great!" Gibby and I found a pay phone—those were still easy to locate in '93—and called Depp.

"Have you seen John?" I asked.

"He's at home. How's your friend?" he said. Johnny didn't know it was River who had been taken away in the ambulance.

"Dude, River's dead!" I told him. There was a long silence, followed by a quiet "Oh, my God . . ." And then the phone went dead.

Well, it was a bit of a relief to know John was back at his house, but of all us, he was the one who could do some real damage. He was the kind of person who would argue—and be serious—that heroin was good for you . . . with a cop. There was no telling what he could say or do. Gibby and I realized just how vulnerable we were. We went back to my apartment and talked all night. The conversation went something like this: "Holy fuck!" We suspected the Los Angeles County Sheriff's Department couldn't wait to start arresting musicians and ac-tors in connection with River's death.

As a jaundiced dawn started to break, Gibby wearily said, "I'm going back home to Texas. I'm booking a flight." He picked up the phone, made a couple calls, and was gone.

Al Jourgensen was on tour and had to leave anyway, and I found out he and his girlfriend had bolted too. I was on my own. By midmorning, the paranoia of sitting alone in my place had started to wear on me, so I went to the Viper Room. It was madness. There was media everywhere. Cameras, reporters, support teams. River's fans had set up makeshift memorials. Red roses, white lilies, and multihued candles colored the dirty sidewalk where not many hours before River had collapsed. I stifled another sob. I loved River, and now he was gone and there wasn't anything I could do.

Junkie self-preservation kicked in. I walked on and found a phone. I called Sal to find out if he had any news. He wasn't happy to hear from me. "Fuck you and fuck your fucking friends, man!" was what he told me. Sal was sober and had a clear picture of what was going on. He knew that the Viper Room was over.

"Where's Johnny?" I asked.

"Johnny's gone, man, and, if I were you, I'd be gone too." Click.

I started to panic. If anyone went down for this, it might be me. I was there. I'd scored drugs the night before. Sal was sober. I wasn't. And now that everyone else had split, I was the only one left here in town. Depressed about River and freaked out for myself, I drove back to my place on La Brea and right in front of my building was a double-parked police prowler. That was not a good sign. I just kept driving.

I hooked a right on Third Street and headed east to the tree-studded hills of Echo Park on the edge of downtown. I didn't know what to do. I went to my old friend Chris Hansen's house and knocked.

He answered the door and I blurted out, "River's dead."

"I know," he said. "It's been all over the news. It's so sad."

"No, dude, you don't understand. I have to get out of town. I need to get to my mom's house in Oklahoma."

I made a few phone calls, booked a flight, and borrowed some money from Chris, and he drove me across town to LAX, where I caught a plane and went to visit my mom, who had, a few years earlier, decided to leave California for the slower pace of the Sooner State. Very few people outside my immediate family knew that, and I thought Oklahoma could provide a safe haven until things calmed down. I was an emotional mess after River's death. I laughed when I should have cried and I wept when I should have laughed. I'd find myself staring at a television set that hadn't been turned on and then realize hours had passed while I sat there as blank as the screen. The Viper Room was done. It wasn't a clubhouse anymore. It was just a place that would forever haunt me with guilt, sadness, and regret—things with which I had become increasingly burdened.

Guilt is a terrible emotion and I'd done a lot of things over the previous decade of which I was ashamed. One thing drugs and alcohol supply is a sort of emotional blankness that allows a person to do the most irresponsible, awful things and hardly give them a thought, but true forgetfulness is an impossibility. Sooner or later, a junkie has to confront himself and the things he's done. On that flight to Oklahoma, I began to catalog all my many fuckups—the failed attempts at sobriety, ego-driven callousness to the people around me, the dope-fiend's innate selfishness. As the miles dragged on, the weight of that list threatened to crush me. I was heartbroken over a lot of things, but one in particular haunted me above all the others.

# MY BOY

As I escaped Los Angeles on my flight to Oklahoma, my mind drifted back to Orange County, California, in 1985. I stared out the window of the jet and saw scenes play out like a movie.

"Would you like another cuppa, love?" the girl said in a High Counties accent, and poured some tea from a china set before she got an answer.

I shot Anthony a look and rolled my eyes. I was drunk.

She passed a plate of cookies across to us. "Biscuits, lads?"

Anthony just smiled and took a macaroon from the plate.

His girl, the one with the posh English accent, perplexed me. Why did she insist on that voice? She was, after all, an Orange County girl. Born and raised right here in the heart of Reagan Country, she and her little group of friends liked musicians.

Anthony, Kendall Jones and Norwood Fisher from Fishbone, and I liked to hang out with pretty young girls. Among this group was a vivacious charmer named Colleen. From my observation, she was the smart one of the pack. Kendall dated her friend. They were giggly girls and often acted silly in a bright and superficial manner that reflected their Orange County environment, especially when Anthony was around. These girls may have liked musicians, but they *loved* Anthony, and they acted goofy and childish whenever he was near. Colleen was different. She had a more mature sensibility. I asked her out, and we spent some time together. I didn't see a future with her. She was healthy, happy, and wholesome. I found that type of woman boring. I wanted drama and excitement. I wanted the kind of woman who would cheat on me with my best friend, and that definitely wasn't Colleen—but she was available, and, like most guys would have, I went for her. In my mind, it was nothing serious. Just a dalliance. I assumed that she was some college chick who had her eyes fixed on a degree. She lived in a nice house in a nice neighborhood with her nice brother. Nice, nice, nice. I slept with her a few times but started to ease myself out of this relationship that, to me, had never existed in any sort of formal state.

One night, I was with Chris Hansen at his place in Echo Park, far, far away from Orange County, fake English accents, brittle macaroons, and nice college girls. The phone screamed out a few times before Chris picked up. I didn't like the look that crossed his face.

"It's for you, Bob."

"Who is it?"

"That girl, Colleen."

"No, no, no, man. Tell her I just left or something."

"Dude. She knows you're here."

He held out the receiver to me like it was a pistol and I needed to do the honorable thing. If he had been a better host, he also would have offered me a blindfold and a last cigarette. I took the receiver from Chris and tentatively said, "Hi, Colleen."

Her voice was calm, like always. "I'm pregnant, Bob. It's your baby."

I was drunk. "Well, what do you expect me to do about it?" A real asshole move, but I was scared. Panicked.

I could hear her start to cry. I hung up the phone. I poured another drink. "I'm going to be a father," I told Chris. As those words sank into my addled brain, I thought that none of this would be too bad. Colleen would have the baby and I'd be a rock star. And I wouldn't have a thing to do with raising a child. Everything would be cool once Colleen got used to the idea.

Her dad had other ideas. While I had convinced myself that Colleen was a college student who lived with her brother and I had constructed this whole backstory about her that I never bothered to verify because I thought I knew it all, that wasn't the case. Not at all.

She was sixteen and a junior in high school.

That house she shared with her brother? It was their parents' place, and Mom and Dad had been on vacation when I visited. I probably should have recognized that two kids wouldn't— couldn't—live in a house like that. And there's no way two kids would have had that kind of taste in furnishings. I had lied to myself because that's what addicts and drunks do. It was a pattern that I tended to repeat.

Just a few months before the Viper Room tragedy I had been

on tour and did a series of dates in Europe. They were club shows, and there was no pressure. The band played tight and I loved the good reviews we got from the music press. I sat on the train between France and Belgium with the black briefcase that held my money, passport, and drugs and caught the eye of a beautiful, young European girl. "Hi, I'm Bob," I said.

"Françoise," she answered back. We made small talk as the train rattled its way to Antwerp.

"You've never been to Antwerp?" she asked, incredulous.

"No, never."

"You must allow me to give you a tour of the city," she said. "It's so beautiful and has much history."

We crossed the flat expanse of the lowlands and pulled into the city and said our good-byes. I promised to call her and then made my way to the hall, where we did our sound check and, later, the show. She was backstage.

"Allo, Bob," she said in her accented English. "Shall we go for a walk?"

I went into the bathroom and did a dose of heroin. I met her outside. We walked and talked almost all night, with frequent pub stops for me. She was a fascinating girl and knew everything about her city. She guided me through cobblestone lanes and wide avenues. We watched the city lights waver in the reflection of the Scheldt River. At a statue in front of the ornate city hall, she told me the story of Antigoon and Brabo, the two characters depicted in the sculpture.

"Antigoon, Bob, was a giant. A terrible giant. And he demanded payment from those who wished to cross the river. Those who could not pay would lose their right hand to Antigoon. Until one day, a hero, Brabo, challenged the giant and killed him. And then he cut off Antigoon's right hand and tossed it as far as he could into the river. Look." She pointed at the statue and there, one in victory and the other in death, both characters were frozen at the dramatic end of her tale. I stumbled a little. "You have maybe had too much to drink, yes? Walk me home and you can stay with me."

This wasn't about sleeping with her, even though she was certainly beautiful. I walked along with her to a quaint street in the heart of the city's diamond district. She led me up the stairs of a beautiful three-story house. I collapsed on the bed, where I dreamed about this flat, lowland country and the tales she had told me weaved in and out of the images. "Bob? Bob?" I heard someone call my name. It took me a moment to realize that I wasn't in a hotel or back in Los Angeles. Françoise scurried around the room as she got dressed. From the light that filtered in through the brocade curtain, I could tell it was early morning. My head hurt and there was the unpleasant taste of last night's booze and cigarettes in my mouth. I groaned and rolled back over and hoped to reenter the dream state. Françoise disapproved of that plan. She shook me. "Bob! You must get up! You cannot stay here! You have to take me to school."

"School?" That jolted me. And as I sat up and fought the rush of nausea that came with the effort, I had a bigger shock. It was hard not to notice that Françoise, this worldly young woman who had given me such an in-depth tour of her city a few hours earlier, was now dressed in a plaid schoolgirl uniform. "What kind of school do you go to?" I asked while the voice in my head screamed, *Please say* college. *Please say* college!

"Why, I go to the finishing school, silly."

*What the fuck is a finishing school?* I wondered. I said, "Well, where I come from, we have school that goes from kindergarten through the twelfth grade. Where does finishing school fall in that range?"

She bit her lower lip and did some mental calculations. Then her face brightened. "Ah, *oui*! I would be in your American eleventh grade!"

This was bad. I had fallen for this girl and here I was a thirty-one-year-old man, alone, in a bedroom with a teenage girl. Maybe it wasn't as bad as I thought. I asked her, "So, how old are you?"

"I'm sixteen."

Not good. Not good at all. My initial guess that Françoise lived in this fancy, three-story home with a couple of girlfriends was seriously off base, and, looking at it now, maybe it was just something I told myself to make the situation seem right. "Whose house is this?" I asked.

"It is my father's house. He's out of town selling diamonds. Get dressed. You have to walk me to school." I swung my feet over the edge of the bed and fumbled with my pants and shirt and pulled on my boots. "Come on, Bob, I'll be late." I stood up and swayed and walked with her down the stairs to the street. As we walked toward her school, we passed the scores of well-dressed Sinjorens—Françoise had taught me that's what the people of Antwerp called themselves—on their way to work or breakfast and silently cursed that I was up at this hour. I had to break it to her. "Look, Françoise, you're a nice girl and everything, but I'm a grown man. This could be really bad for me."

We hauled up next to her school, where dozens of young girls giggled and chatted about young-girl things. I felt a little sick. "Don't worry, Bob. I'll be seventeen in a few weeks. Then I will be . . . a grown woman."

"Well, that's good to know. I have to be going now."

"Good-bye, Bob." She scribbled something on a piece of paper, shoved it into my hand, and gave me a quick kiss. "Call me," she said, and skipped off past the iron gates that marked the perimeter of the school. I shoved the paper into my coat pocket and walked back to the train station. "This is bad. This is so bad," I muttered to myself, but I knew how it would play out. I had fallen for her.

We continued with the tour and I called her every chance I could. I fucked up everybody's schedule by disappearing to Antwerp whenever I could. The great thing about Europe is that it's small. Nothing is ever too far away. The tour was set to go through Amsterdam, and Françoise wanted in on the deal. "I want to come with you, Bob. Please, take me along." How could I say no? Besides, she was, as they'd say back home, "legal" now.

She came with a girlfriend and they got set up in the hotel. By this time, I didn't hide anything from her and she saw me using heroin. "What is that, Bob?"

"Heroin."

"I want to try it."

"No. Are you crazy?"

"Bob, I want to know what you know. Feel what you feel. I am your girlfriend."

"No."

"You are so mean sometimes." She pouted and crossed her arms. "A good boyfriend would not act like this."

I had some East Asian heroin and I parceled out a little

mound on a glass-topped table. I eyeballed it and tried to gauge the right amount of the dull white powder that would give her a taste but not be too heavy or dangerous. I crushed it with the lid of a Zippo lighter and then chopped it with the edge of a credit card and drew out a thin line. I figured this would be just the right amount for her, but drugs are not always an exact science. I blew it badly. I handed her a rolled-up bill that looked like it came from a Monopoly game and watched as she dipped her head to the table and sniffed it up with a quick, hard snort. She sat up straight with a triumphant smile on her face and looked at me. I returned her gaze and was horrified as I watched her serenity turn to panic just before her lids fluttered and eyes rolled back. She went down. I'd misjudged badly. Overdose.

I dragged her limp form into the bathroom and put her under a cold shower. There was a wall-mounted phone in there and I dialed 911. I didn't learn until later that, in Europe, the emergency code is 112. I was not equipped to deal with this situation and Françoise needed help. I called the front desk. "I have a medical emergency! Send help!"

"Yes, do not worry, sir," came the disembodied response from the other end of the line.

I felt for a pulse on Françoise's neck and found it. It was faint, but her heart still pumped. I kept the cold water from the shower on and made sure it ran over her unconscious frame. It seemed like hours, but within minutes there was powerful knock at the door. I let in the Dutch emergency crew.

"She's in the shower," I said.

They went in and got to work. It was obvious that they had done this before. I freaked out. Here I was in a foreign country, with a young girl who had overdosed on the drugs I had supplied. There was no way, I thought, that this scene would end well. But I was wrong. Just like I didn't know the emergency phone number in Europe, I also didn't know that, at least in Amsterdam, once the paramedics resuscitate those unfortunate enough to suffer an overdose, they pack up their equipment and leave. No police, no doctors, no hospitals. It's just "Good luck, kiddo. We've got to go." And, like them, I had to go too. Sound check, show, next town. I parted company with Françoise, but I didn't forget her. The tour became increasingly fucked up as I did everything I could to get back to Antwerp whenever the opportunity arose.

It's how I found myself back, unannounced, on her doorstep one night. I rang the bell. No answer. I knocked. No answer. I looked up and saw no lights. It was early evening, so I planned to wait. I had to see her. I went to wait in the pub across the street and started to drink. We had just played the big Pinkpop Festival in Landgraaf, the Netherlands, on a bill with Living Colour, Lenny Kravitz, Rage Against the Machine, and the Black Crowes in front of more than sixty thousand people. I made a spectacle of myself at that show. I felt hopeless about the way things were. My plan was to kill myself onstage and become a famous rock-and-roll suicide. In front of all those people, I'd climb to the top of one of the rigging scaffolds and take a swan dive. But when I got up there and looked down, I chickened out. *Fuck, that's a long drop,* I thought. I came back down as the band played and then went through my usual front-man histrionics once I got back onstage. I finished up the show by cursing Jesus. It felt right because the festival was held on Pentecost weekend. The crowd loved it. Our show was written about extensively in the European press. I was a celebrity and everyone in that bar wanted to buy a drink for the crazy, tortured artist. I accepted their kindness, but I didn't really feel like talking to any of them. I kept walking outside to see if Françoise had come home. She hadn't.

I went back inside for more pats on the back and more drinks from the locals. I started to chat with an older man. He was cultured and smart and I got along with him. He wasn't like the rest of the crowd, who seemed unduly impressed that I had been in the press. We both kept drinking and, as will often happen in a drinking bout, we became best buddies four rounds in. But Françoise was still on my mind, and I walked outside again. My new friend followed me out and saw me peering at the houses across the street.

"Bob, my friend, at what do you look?"

I took a pull from my cigarette and launched into my story. "There's a girl I'm in love with."

"Ah, yes, love."

"Well, she lives across the street. I'm waiting for her to get home."

"This girl. What house is she in?"

"That one right there," I said, and pointed.

A look crossed his face. Maybe he knew her. Maybe not. "This girl of yours. What is her name?"

"Françoise," I said.

"Françoise?" He burst out in a laugh and embraced me. "That girl is my daughter!"

That I wasn't murdered on the spot impressed me. "I love Europe!" I said. But Françoise didn't come home and I had to get on the road and finish the tour. Back home, I tried to keep in touch, but being separated by a continent and an ocean makes the logistics difficult. It wasn't like I could hop a train. What can I say? The truth is I like younger women. I always have.

But Colleen's dad didn't have a European outlook on my relationship with his daughter. Neither did the district attorney. This was serious business and I was threatened with statutory rape charges. I was dragged into the state of California's legal system and I became—officially—a father. I was also ordered to pay child support once the baby arrived. It was a heartbreaking situation. Colleen faced her pregnancy alone. If she harbored hatred toward me, she never showed it. I was all set to do what friends of mine had done when faced with similar circumstances: run. The district attorney and the state of California made sure I didn't. I wrote a song about it that appeared on *Next Saturday Afternoon*. I called it "Hang Tough."

*Got up this morning to go to court*
*The DA started telling me, "It's time to grow up."*

To hang tough and be responsible to Colleen and the imminent arrival of our baby became my goal. There was a problem, though. Despite my noble, court-ordered intentions, I was in no kind of shape to take on that sort of role. The drugs and drink had too great a hold on me, and even the birth of a child wouldn't be enough to loosen their grip.

Colleen gave birth in 1986 to a boy child and he was named Elijah. I tried my best to make the trip to Orange County to visit every month. I tried my best to pay what I could for his support. I tried to be a dad . . . and I came up short. I was a 10 percent father to him. I justified it in my head by telling myself that Colleen had several good men who were her friends and they could fill in the blanks that I left. It wasn't as if Elijah wouldn't have good role models, I told myself, and, despite my absenteeism, I loved that kid. When I'd see him, I was fascinated by the little critter. I would watch him play and think, *Oh, my God! He's just like me!* It blew my mind, and yet, I still didn't get it. I couldn't get it. Even now, today, I don't remember a lot of that time. I must have changed a diaper at some point, but I can't recall doing it. I must have given him a bottle, but I draw a blank on that. I wasn't healthy enough to be a parent, and Colleen knew it.

If I was in a good period and not completely incoherent on drugs and the party life, Colleen and Elijah would come up to visit. If I was on really good behavior, they might even spend the night. But it wasn't until 1989, after my first attempt at sobriety, that I was allowed to keep him by myself for a weekend. I might have gaps in my memory about Elijah's early life, but I remember that weekend.

"Now, I wrote down his schedule, Bob. Just check that if you need to. All the important phone numbers are there too. His stuff's in this bag." Colleen handed me the satchel and left while a little wide-eyed toddler looked up at me, as if to say, "Well, what now, Pops?"

I didn't have a clue. We played, we ate, we watched cartoons, and the whole time he was with me, I was fascinated and terrified. When it was time to put him to sleep, I had the awful fear of him falling out of bed. I went through the house like a crazy person and grabbed every pillow and blanket I could to build a little fortress around him. He survived the night and the rest of the weekend. It felt like a milestone, and I started taking him maybe twice a month.

But I still didn't get it. In my family, money was important. It was what conferred comfort and status, and while it wasn't love, it was the closest thing to it. If I bought Elijah things, and if I paid what the court had deemed appropriate, I was a good father. Then I witnessed what a real father does when Flea had his daughter. He was an on-site parent from his little pad in the Fairfax District. It wasn't the lap of luxury, but he set the bar high as a father. I wanted to be like him, but I couldn't.

I was fucked up all the time, and one night, in one of those pensive doper moods, I had the brilliant flash that I wasn't doing myself any good and I certainly wasn't doing Elijah any good. He had come to visit me in rehab when he was four. It was awful. Every attempt to clean up involved a group session where the dads would talk about their children.

We'd sit in that circle, and I'd hear the laments and the boasts.

"My kids are the most important things in my life," said one guy.

"I'd do anything for my children," swore another.

I'd sit with my arms folded and think, *What a bunch of bullshit.* I wanted to shout, "If your kids meant that much to you, you wouldn't be getting high. You'll do anything for your kids as long as it doesn't involve giving up drugs and booze." My way seemed like the best path. Just disappear. Stay out of the kid's life. Now I can't help but think I was just a selfish asshole.

In 1996, after two dozen rides on the rehab-go-round, I felt like I was ready to reconnect. My girlfriend Max called Colleen.

"Bob's sober. He really wants to see Elijah."

"Oh, really? Just like the last twenty-four times?"

"He feels awful."

"Well, Elijah's got a baseball game. Tell Bob he can come to that."

I was excited. I couldn't wait. I was six weeks sober and Elijah was nine years old. It was April and the start of the Little League season. The kids all had little mock-ups of baseball cards with their pictures on the front and stats on the back. Elijah solemnly handed one to me. I kept that thing in my wallet for years. I'd look at it and it would make me cry for the years I'd lost. I started to attend all his games. By July, Colleen must have seen a change in me. Elijah started to come stay with me in my little apartment some weekends.

One day Colleen called me. "How would you like to have Elijah for the month?"

My first impulse was to panic and say, "I can't handle something like that!" but then I remembered some advice I had just been given by a counselor as part of my recovery. "Bob, you say no to everything. It's time you start to say yes."

I caught myself and stammered into the phone, "B-bring him over." Every instinct I had told me this was the wrong thing to do—I was still unsure about my sobriety—but I went with it. The visit went well and I felt as if I'd contributed to the greater good. Colleen had just started a relationship that would eventually lead to a long-term marriage. Up until then, from the time she was a girl, she had been a mother to a small child with a mostly absent, drug-addicted father. The poor girl needed to start her own life. I suggested, not long after that initial monthlong stay, that Elijah come and stay with me for a semester while he attended school. I worked and was a real dad for the first time in my life. It felt good. Elijah had two sets of actively involved parents . . . which couldn't have been easy for him. When he got in trouble at school for some little infraction, we would all go down to the school for a conference.

But I worried. I could see so much of me in that kid. At eleven, he was reading William Faulkner and understanding him. And I was convinced that I had passed along an ill-defined, unhealthy mental gene. He could be a wiseass and a know-it-all, just like me. On the other hand, I could also see he was a gentleman and was kind and tolerant. He also loved music, and as he became a man, he got more into that.

He's one of the most talented songwriters I know. He performs under the name Terrors. Of course, the music of his generation is different from the music of mine. He writes beautiful songs, but he performs them in a lo-fi style that makes it difficult to hear the lyrics. I tell him to lose the reverb and the distortion. He looks at me and smiles. I hope someday to record an album of his tunes, *Songs My Son Wrote*.

Like any father, I want him to be rewarded for his talent like I was for mine. For ten years, I had money, I traveled the world . . . and I didn't have to have a regular job. Not long ago, Elijah accompanied me on guitar as I sang the first song I ever wrote about him, "My Boy," which appeared on Thelonius Monster's 1990 album *Stormy Weather*.

*My boy, well, I've never even held you in my arms, boy*
*But you're my boy*
*My boy, well, I've only seen you*
*I've only seen you once or twice, boy, oh*
*But you're my boy, and one day you and me, boy*
*We're gonna have it out, yeah,*

*One day you and me, boy*
*We're gonna have it out, yeah,*
*And I know you'll probably hate me*
*But that's life, boy, my boy, yeah*

I was moved and I cried. When we finished, he said to me, "I never hated you like you thought in that song, Dad. You were a good father . . . when you were around." But all too often, I wasn't. I was incapable. It was the drugs and the drink, and the scene only continued to grow darker.

# ARISE, LAZARUS, AND WALK!

J ohn Frusciante had always had a reputation for following his own special beat—and for being a major endorser of any and every drug known to man, woman, or child. He was artistic and he could be sensitive. For a short time, he sat in on guitar with my band Thelonious Monster, but after Hillel Slovak died from an overdose on June 25, 1988, John joined the Red Hot Chili Peppers. Lately, I had become concerned about my old friend. I hadn't gone around his place much since the Viper Room days of a few years earlier. The tragedy of that night and the ever-increasing air of weirdness at John's had kept me away to a degree. But I had heard things. Some of them unbelievable. It was 1996 and I was pretty sure he'd hadn't left his Hollywood Hills pad in months. He'd been surviving on drop-offs and deliveries. Most of those, I'm sure, came packed in Ziploc bags from any number of sources that cultivated and catered to an exclusive celebrity clientele and helped them to get by. Given my own continuing go-rounds with under-the-counter pharmaceuticals, it wasn't my place to judge John, but some of the things I'd heard about him were disconcerting. Most people don't hold all-night conversations with the ghost of Joy Division's Ian Curtis, which manifested its ectoplasmic presence out of one of John's stereo speakers. I thought it might be a good idea to go to see how John was doing . . . or at least check to see that he wasn't in what a medical examiner might call "a state of mottled decomposition."

Following the same protocol from the Viper Room days, I traced a circuitous route to John's house. I'm not sure why I did this. It wasn't as if I was afraid of prying eyes at this point. I wheeled into the driveway and stood for a moment to take in the dry, medicinal smell of eucalyptus that scented the air. John's house looked pretty much the same as always. The lawn and the landscaping had recently been tended. If he had passed into the Great Beyond, somebody was still paying the gardeners. And I knew it wasn't Ian Curtis's shade.

The door creaked open when I pushed. Do you know those public-service TV commercials with an antidrug message that always show a doper's pad as some dimension of hell straight out of a Bosch painting? John's place was worse. The squalor was alive and crawling, and I walked straight into a wall of foul smells as soon as my feet crossed the threshold. The furniture didn't just have cigarette burns—the telltale spoor of the nodded-off junkie—there was a mattress that had been pulled into one corner that looked as if someone had tried to construct a pit barbecue in its center. Bottles containing liquids the origins of which I didn't even want to guess were strewn on the floor. Not that I would look down on him. This was, when you come right down to it, pretty normal for the way lots of junkies live, but Frusciante was doing it big and taking it to new and dangerous levels. This verged on performance art, the kind where no one gets out alive.

He shambled into the front room and didn't look surprised to see me at all. He nodded and said, "Hey, man. I was thinking about you." He wore the terminal addict's waxen, gray pallor over his sunken cheeks. I'd seen that face before in my own mirror, but, like his pad, this was beyond the beyond. The effort it took to acknowledge me left him winded. It looked like his body was consuming itself to maintain the stasis of its high.

It was John's own treatment program. He said he had kicked heroin cold-turkey—an impressive feat, no doubt—but he still smoked crack on a perpetual cycle and drank heroic amounts of alcohol. His eyes glittered maniacally from a skull framed with lank, brittle hair. His arms, from years of needle abuse, were a gnarled mess of old abscesses and healed-over wens. When he smiled, his teeth showed through black.

There was one thing that didn't fit. John wore the typical crackhead drag: a sweater that looked moth-eaten, jeans falling from the place where he used to have hip bones . . . What didn't compute were his boots. They were brand-new pearl-gray lace-ups with lavender and green leather inlays. They stood out because I knew he could only have bought these boots in London. They came from a little shop on Carnaby Street. I remembered a day in 1992 when John and I met over coffee at Denny's on Sunset and I had seen him wearing them; he had told me to buy a pair the next time I was in London. Seeing this footwear confused me. Had this walking-dead junkie somehow managed to board a plane and fly halfway around the globe to buy a new pair of boots? I asked him, "You been to London lately?"

He followed my eyes to his boots. "No, Bob, these are the same boots."

"They can't be. They would be, like, five years old."

"They are. I just wear 'em here. I haven't been outside in a while."

"Man, you should get out. Check out your yard. Your gardeners have knocked themselves out."

I would have been amused by this dazed and confused small talk, but my friend was crashing as a viable living organism in front of my eyes. The footwear might have concerned me, but his eyes terrified me. He was twenty-seven years old, and he had a look that recalled every old man with senile dementia I had ever passed on the streets of Hollywood. Whatever candles burned behind those eyes were fluttering out. Not many years earlier we'd shared a sort of punk rock bravado about our favorite rock stars who'd died young—Gram Parsons, Brian Jones, Jimi Hendrix, Jim Morrison. Seeing John's life and spirit exit in curls of smoke from the glass pipe scared me. I saw all my illusions about cool, success, fame, and having a good time die. John wasn't just my friend. He had a true gift as a guitar player. And it was all going up in crack smoke. I couldn't fully admit to the depths of my own problems, but I could see John's with crystal clarity. I had to do something. He was becoming mummified in this place. I knew if he stayed here any longer, he was going to die.

"Man, don't your teeth hurt?" I asked.

He nodded and palmed his jaw. Of course they did. If you neglect yourself long enough, your teeth are the first things to go. You smoke enough crack, your teeth rot out from the smoke and lack of saliva. Oddly enough, he was in a place where the thing that might really kill him wasn't drugs but an infection from his derelict, abcessed teeth.

My reaching out to him from a place of understanding worked. I was surprised that he was willing. I guess he was done. We walked out to my Jeep. "Wow. You're right," he said, blinking like a deep-sea creature pulled too fast to the surface. "Those bougainvilleas look great." It was, no doubt, the first time his boots had touched the gravel walkway in years. One of the gardening crew, an older Mexican, had just walked around a corner of the house and stopped dead in his tracks at the sight of this wan apparition who looked a lot like Saint Lazarus. The only thing missing was a dog to lick John's hands.

We got into my Jeep. I picked up my cell phone to call Las Encinas Hospital. John looked perplexed. "What's that?" he asked.

"It's a cell phone. They've been around for a while now, John." I guess he'd been so isolated he hadn't seen one before.

When I dropped him off at Las Encinas and saw the staff of chirpy people walk him in, I felt like I'd delivered him to a new and better life. This was the motherfucker of all good deeds. I really cared about him and I had pulled him from death's door.

*I must be a pretty good person,* I thought. I was in my Jeep driving onto the 101 freeway and on autopilot, I turned back toward John's house. My next thought was, *I bet he has a bunch of shit in his house. No sense in letting it go to waste. I'm going to get high.*

145

Once back at John's place, I didn't have any trouble locating his stash. I used it to cook up a crack rock the size of a baseball. To me, it was a work of art. It almost seemed a shame to break off a chunk and destroy its pristine roundness, but that's exactly what I did. I shoved the ivory-colored chip into a glass tube that had one end stuffed with a filter made from a copper scouring pad. I brought it to my lips, held a flame to the rock, and inhaled deeply. I heard the sizzle and pop as it melted and felt the smoke numb my tongue and throat. I held it in for as long as I could and then exhaled a cartoonishly huge billow of white smoke. I watched it expand and felt my heart start to race while I heard my blood pulse through my ears before the hit slammed into the front part of my brain and lit up every conceivable pleasure receptor.

I didn't think of this as "stealing." Junkies never do.

There's an old story in recovery meetings that goes, "The difference between a drunk and a junkie is this: An alkie will steal your wallet. A junkie will steal your wallet and then help you look for it." That's the kind of friend I was. Everything boiled down to that one sputtering rock in the pipe.

I was at the tail end of a dark period, and I was bone-tired of the life I had been living. The years 1993 through 1995 were a blurry, bleary-eyed mess that I would just as soon have forgotten if they hadn't left such a hard stamp on me. They'd wrecked me and shamed me. There had been that awful moment in January of 1993 when I sang the national anthem at a Clippers game at the Los Angeles Memorial Sports Arena. I had been asked to perform the song, and I was a Clippers fan. What could possibly go wrong? I drank heavily and smoked some crack to sharpen up before I went in front of the crowd. I had the idea to sing the song as a slow, folkish antiwar protest tune. I think I was the first punk rocker to have ever been asked to sing the national anthem at any American sporting event. Clipper Ron Harper even gave me a little pat on the ass like jocks do at games in anticipation of what was sure to be a stirring and thought-provoking opening to the game. "Go get 'em, Bob!"

"Ladies and gentlemen, please rise for the singing of the national anthem, tonight being performed by Bob Forrest!" The crowd gave me a huge ovation. I walked out to my mark and faced the microphone. I stood on the waxed and polished hard-wood floor and started the song.

*Oh, say can you see . . .*

I blew it. Badly. I forgot the words. I froze. I had to start over. My throat was tight and my voice sounded strained. The song was a complete mess and the crowd started to boo me. Their cries became deafening. Paper cups and trash were tossed at me. Ron Harper shook his head in disgust. It was an utter embarrassment. I could sense some real hatred in the stands. The Clippers lost and a lot of people felt my performance had jinxed the team. I was seen as "anti-American" and disrespect-ful. In the parking lot, after the game, two marines approached.

"Hey, dude, good song," the bigger one said.

"Wow. Cool. I'm glad you guys got what I was trying to do."

"He didn't mean you sang it good. He meant that the song is good," said his buddy, a squat, muscular guy who resembled one of those little dorm refrigerators.

"Yeah," said his bigger friend. "We'd give our lives for that song, and we don't appreciate some dumb-ass getting up there and making fun of it."

"That's not what I—"

Before I could finish, I caught a roundhouse left in the jaw and went down hard on the asphalt, the heels of my palms scraped raw on the rough surface. I tried to get back up but was hit again in the temple. I heard the dull thud as the blow crashed into my skull. It was plain I couldn't fight these two, so I curled up and tried to protect my head and vitals as best I could. They stomped me with their hard-soled shoes. It was as quick and brutal a beat-down as any ever given in a prison exercise yard, and it left me dazed, bruised, and reeling. The next day, out on the street as I made my way to the corner liquor store, it felt like every eye that passed was on me. A dog approached me. "Do you want to bite me?" I asked it sarcastically. It just stood there with one of those goofy dog smiles on its face. It gave a friendly bark and wagged its tail. "Ah, well, here's a creature that just takes me for who I am. You don't hate me, do ya, boy?" I bent down to give it a pet. "Good doggie," I said. The pooch and I had a nice moment of heart-to-heart communication until its owner saw me and shouted, "Get the fuck away from my dog, man! I saw what you did last night, you rotten little fucker! I fought in Vietnam, for cryin' out loud! I ought to get my gun and put one in your noodle, creep!" It had come to the point where I couldn't even pet a mangy mutt in the street without drawing somebody's anger. It was dispiriting and I was exhausted. Little did I realize that there was worse to come.

By 1995, I was essentially homeless and I crashed on peoples' couches. I sold drugs for dealers I knew just to keep myself high. People died around me. It was a rootless existence and my life was in a complete shambles. There were people who offered to help. Big James was a guy in Los Angeles who was the ultimate Thelonious Monster fan. A huge, hulking lump of a man, he'd go into near paroxysms of delight when he'd come to our shows and he was always thrilled to talk to me. He took me in, but room and board—like everything else in this world—came with a price. Big James liked to party and he liked music, and with me under his roof, he hit upon an idea: living room concerts that featured the front man from his favorite band. He had easy access since I stayed in his spare room.

"You're putting on a show tonight, Bob!" he said enthusiastically one late afternoon, a big goofy grin plastered across his face.

"What?" I asked, not sure I had heard him right. I hadn't been booked anywhere. Had I forgotten a gig? Not likely.

"Yeah, it's all set up. A bunch of my friends are going to come over and you're going to play. It'll be awesome!"

"Uh, I don't know, man," I said. I had things to do. Drugs to take. Friends' cars to crash. Some kind of trouble waited for me out on the streets and I didn't want to miss the appointment and be stuck here putting on a half-assed, rinky-dink show in some guy's living room. I wasn't in the mood. I was a rock star. I played real-life, honest-to-goodness concerts. I didn't do stupid stuff like this. I mean, the Red Hot Chili Peppers didn't perform in some guy's squalid and festering living room for a bunch of jokers who couldn't find anyplace better to go to drink cheap beer on a Friday night.

"Well, you are kind of staying here for free, man," Big James said. A look of hurt and disappointment clouded his usually sunny face. "It wouldn't exactly kill you to contribute a little," he said, pouting.

He had me there. He was a good cat and he would lend me money when I asked. Big James fed me. It didn't feel right to take from the guy without giving something in return. Besides, I thought, where else did I have to go? Was I really prepared to sleep in an alley under a soggy cardboard packing crate with only the crook of my arm for a pillow? That didn't really strike me as a great alternative, so I became Big James's dancing, singing rock-and-roll marionette. A punk-rock sock puppet. His glassy-eyed friends rolled in, beer drinkers and hell-raisers, and sat around the living room on the cup-cushioned couch and the sway-backed, threadbare chairs while I thrummed away at my guitar and sang my songs like some drug-damaged and deranged cabaret chanteuse. Halfway through what passed for my set, some guy held up a Bic lighter and shouted, "Play some Skynyrd, dude!"

*This is like the twilight of the gods,* I thought. *I live in a fan's house and I play concerts in the living room.* Big James loved it. "The guy from Thelonious Monster stays at my house!" he'd bellow. "Fuck yeah!"

It was a comedown. A big one. In 1993, Thelonious Monster had played before tens of thousands of screaming, can't-get-enough rock music fans, and now here I was croaking out my songs in front of a crowd of tens made up of a bunch of slack-jawed goobers and voyeuristic gawkers who probably cringed at what they saw. If they remembered the old Bob, this was his comeuppance. It felt like some cruel cosmic payback for some transgression I couldn't even remember. What could I have done to deserve this? I could see the writing on the wall, the signpost up ahead, the "No Exit" warning. Things were headed toward an ugly, spectacular crash on the dead-end street of my life.

# REDEMPTION

On February 3, 1996—the thirty-seventh anniversary of the deaths of Buddy Holly, the Big Bopper, and Ritchie Valens in a rock-and-roll plane crash—I found myself on rain-slicked city streets in front of Hollywood Moguls, a then-popular nightclub with a façade that resembled, with no weak sense of irony, a decrepit tin toolshed. Traffic lights and headlamps shined on the pebbled mirror of wet asphalt and a cold, sickly rainbow of red, green, yellow, and white reflected back toward a starless sky. The holidays were a month past and although the rest of the city had fallen back into its routine, you couldn't have guessed from the boisterous club-goers who clogged the sidewalk and bunched up at the door. With a certain crowd, the festivities never ended. And here I was, broke, hungry, down on my luck, but with a firm grip on the invisible keys to every door of the city's underground as well as its celebrity haunts. I was on the hunt for a soft touch. This was a pattern I had established whenever money got tight, and it was tighter than a firmly clenched fist at the moment. I knew where everybody hung out, and with a little luck, I wouldn't have to make too many stops before I could spot a friendly face who would let me borrow some cash. Credit cards and checks are worthless currency when you want to buy drugs, and I needed something quick.

Since my earliest days on the club scene, I'd known how to get in a door. I never paid a cover charge and I never waited in line. Tonight was no different. I pushed my way to the front of the line and the doorman recognized me. We exchanged nods.

"Go on in, Bob," said the huge gorilla who guarded the gate.

"I don't think I'll be here long," I told him, speaking the plain truth as I squeezed between him and the wall.

Inside the club were knots of party people who crowded the floor and the bar. The electronic music pummeled me and I could feel the vibrations from the subwoofers rattle my guts. In my current condition, it wasn't a pleasant sensation. I felt like I might hurl whatever I had stored in there, although it couldn't have been much since I had hardly eaten over the past week. I headed for the VIP area and got past the red velvet rope. I did a quick scan and noticed my friend Perry Farrell of Jane's Addiction sitting in a corner. Dope-sick and covered with a thin sheen of sweat, I struck up a conversation with him and, with little time to waste, hit him up.

"Uh, say, man, do you think you could let me borrow maybe thirty or forty bucks?" I asked.

Perry was no fool. I could tell right away that he knew what was up and why I needed quick cash, but he showed some mercy and reached into a pocket and said, "I only have hundreds, Bob. Here, take this." He handed me a crisp note. I ignored the sad—maybe disgusted—look on his face and I snatched the bill with the quickness of a rattlesnake strike.

"Thanks, Perry. I'll get you back on this real soon." I could tell that as soon as my fingers touched that money, he had written it off as gone for good. He was probably right. I didn't have time to dwell on it or even bother to make small talk with my savior. "Uh, I have to run, man," I said, and I quickly made it out to the street, where I had parked a new Ford Escort wagon. It belonged to a chick named Sandy, who was the girlfriend of an out-of-town drug dealer. I had told her I only needed it for an hour and here I had already been gone for three. Drug time is different from any other time you'll ever know. Sometimes it's slow and sometimes it's fast, but it never, ever has any relationship to actual minutes on a clock. I fumbled the keys with locked-up fingers and slid behind the steering wheel. The Escort's little four-banger chugged to life and I pulled away from the curb as fast as I could. There was no time to waste and the money I had gotten from Perry was my passport to a better place. But before I got there, I had to travel through purgatory. I drove east on wet surface streets to the intersection of Seventh and Alvarado, just west of downtown.

This was MacArthur Park, a place made famous by song-writer Jimmy Webb in his odd orchestral elegy to the city. The line "someone left the cake out in the rain" still has the power to confuse listeners, but anyone who has ever taken a nighttime stroll along the edge of the park's artificial lake and scuffled through the ammoniated waste produced by the huge flocks of waterfowl that skim, dive, and float on its murky surface and ride the sullen and slow currents that pile up the slag on the lake's concrete shore knows exactly what Webb meant. MacArthur Park had always been an underground marketplace where dedicated searchers could find what they needed, provided they had cash. Fake IDs, Social Security cards, sex, steamed tamales, and any kind of drug known to humankind were on sale and priced to move in those dim shadows. Of course, it was also the kind of place where the unwary and foolish could just as easily be killed as complete a transaction. I wasn't worried. I knew how to be careful, although $100 was more than enough to get me into trouble. But sometimes, you just have to have a little trust in your fellow man.

It didn't take me long to find some Mexican kid in baggy khakis and an oversized plaid Pendleton shirt who was slinging. He knew I was a shopper. "What you need, *ese*?" he asked. I smiled. We conducted our business in a matter of seconds, all communication done by nods, hand gestures, and quickly flashed goods. No need for fake niceties; we both knew the routine and played our parts well. It was time to go, and I trotted back to the car while the kid slipped back into the shadows. I started to pull away from the curb and into the sparse traffic when I saw that a cop car was parked on the other side of the street. He had to have known what a white boy like me was up to in this open-air drug emporium after dark. The chase was on, but, because we were on opposite sides of the street and faced different directions, he had to make a U-turn to get back around and make the stop. By that time, I was gone. That little Ford Escort was maneuverable. I turned off the headlights, swung onto a side street, and made a series of quick turns before I doubled back. This is where I fucked up. I probably should have driven to a well-traveled street like Pico and headed west, but, well, I wasn't thinking clearly. Instead, I thought I'd be slick. I parked the car, got out, and started to walk. Big mistake. I was busted almost immediately. "Sir, could you step over here, please?" Sometimes the Los Angeles cops can be so courteous. At the same time they explicitly telegraph that they think you're a scumbag.

"What's the problem, officer?" I asked with as much unctuous middle-class charm as I could manage.

"Just shut it and put your hands on the car," he said. I balanced myself with the palms of my hands flat on the trunk of the cruiser as the cop kicked my legs back and apart. He did a pat-down and came up with my newly purchased bag of dope. "And what do we have here?" he asked. He knew the answer, and there was no point in any further remarks from me. "Put your hands behind your back," he said, and I was slapped into the cuffs. He walked me around the side of the car and opened the rear door. "Watch your head, sir," he said, and then stuffed me inside like a pile of dirty laundry. And that was that. I was caught and it was time to take a little ride. As we drove, I noticed we weren't bound for downtown. That could only mean one possible destination—the notorious Rampart station, a place that had a well-deserved reputation for busting heads.

Now, in gangster movies and TV shows, the advice is always, "Just shut up until your lawyer arrives." This is a great tip in principle, but I didn't have an attorney on retainer and cops who think you're being a wiseass can make sure you get put into a cell with some serious dudes who will lay upon you a beat-down or worse. As soon as they brought me in to the booking desk, I used another little piece of advice I had gleaned somewhere along the way. The first words out of my mouth, before I even confirmed my name, were, "I'm gay. I going to need protection." The booking officer looked at me—maybe with disbelief, it was hard to tell—but he didn't have any choice but to take me at my word. That's how it works. Once you've dropped that little bomb on them, they reroute you through protective custody and keep you away from the general jail population. Apparently, homosexuals are disruptive to what passes for serenity in "gen pop." The squalid accommodations at Rampart weren't any better for those of us in protective custody, but under the auspices of "PC," I didn't have to worry—as much, anyway—about the specter of random and sudden violence. I had a bigger concern: withdrawal. This was not the time or place to be dope-sick, given the upcoming court appearances and the stress of incarceration, but that was the reality.

Because of my protective-custody status, I was sent downtown to the "Glass House" facility at Parker Center instead of the nightmarish Men's Central Jail. Not that any correctional facility is a good place to be, but Men's Central can be downright lethal. I can't recall much of my stay in the Glass House. The processing routine is designed to strip the inmate of whatever shred of dignity he might still possess. Everything is delivered in a stream of sharply barked orders by some jarhead sheriff's deputy.

"Strip!"

"Walk on the blue lines *only!*"

"Bend over!"

"Cough!"

"Lift your nut sack and cough again!"

Then you get a shower and some ill-fitting clothes. It passed in a blur. I was as dope-sick as any junkie's ever been, and the county doesn't give you any methadone. You take the cure right there in lockup. After a few days of wrenching intestinal conniptions, I started to feel physically better, but I didn't have the luxury to reflect on it. Hauled before a judge, I was put on a big, black-and-white sheriff's department bus and sent to a facility called Wayside in the dusty foothills of Castaic. It was called the "honor rancho" and it was laid out as a group of low-slung buildings that baked in the near-constant daytime sunshine and froze during the clear and cloudless nights. I found myself in a dormitory situation with the other sad-sack miscreants who had drawn the protective-custody card. And there we sat with not much to do but go to court and complain to each other about what a drag it was to be locked up. On the plus side, nobody got raped or shanked. I cooled there for thirty days, which gave me the time to clear up old warrants. Unfortunately, I learned I was also being charged with grand theft auto.

Sandy, the girl who had, perhaps unwisely, let me borrow her newly purchased Ford Escort, was completely pissed off in the aftermath of my arrest. I can't say that I blame her. I had carelessly left her car on the street and I never had the common courtesy to call her from jail. As a result, her beloved and recently purchased ride was considered abandoned and it was impounded by the city in one of the vast lots where machines go to die. Because she didn't have any money to get it out, it stayed there accruing fines until it was finally repossessed. As might be understandable—to anyone but me at the time—Sandy wanted payback, and so, to inflict maximum damage on me for my transgression, she alleged that I had stolen her car. Fortunately, I was released on my own recognizance and was able to clear up that mess on the outside. I made a beeline to her as soon as I was out.

"What the fuck, Sandy?"

"I lost my fucking car, Bob."

"But I was going to cop dope for both of us."

"Bullshit, man. I never would have seen any of that. And now my credit's fucked up and I don't have a car."

"Well, I'm sorry about that, but, look, I'm staring down some time because you're mad at me. That doesn't seem right, does it?"

"I don't care what happens to you. You fucked me over."

"What if I promise to make things up? Set it all right? Cover your expenses? I can't go to prison for something like this. It was all a mistake. I'm sorry!"

Those two words, *I'm sorry,* have a lot of power. She agreed. We cleared things up between us and, more importantly, eventually, between me and the state of California. In the greater picture, the one in which I saw my conflated self-image shrinking by the moment, I had an epiphany. *I'm clean,* I thought. *I'm finally fucking clean.* I hadn't been in a long time, although I had made numerous, ultimately failed, attempts. It was a revelation. The thirty days I had spent locked up had forced me to take a hard, brutal look at my life and my problems. I couldn't keep going back to rehab. Since that first time at Hazelden, I'd clean up for a while, fall back into using, get talked into another stab at rehab, and then fail again. I was on an endless rehab roller coaster, and the cure never took. I just loved drugs too much. It was just self-defeating. It didn't work for me, obviously. This should have been clear to me after the first go-round at Hazelden, but I had been in twenty-six programs in total, and I was still a junkie and an alcoholic.

Now, this might come as a shock to somebody who's never run with monsters, but after that many attempts at self-help—and each one followed by a failure—the despair adds up and starts to demand a price. In my case, it was ego. I couldn't look at myself in the mirror without seeing the sad and pathetic clown who stared back at me. It was the same joker who had always been there, but for the first time, I saw him with a degree of clarity and perspective. Twenty-six times in rehab? Was it even possible to be more ridiculous? I was a fool. A jester. A buffoon. The clown of the crack pipe. And that hurt. This time, it was going to be different.

I started to attend recovery meetings again. Sheepishly, at first. I viewed some of the philosophies and concepts with skepticism and disdain—the whole business about a benevolent and all-knowing "power" is still something I have trouble with—but I kept at it because, after so many screwups and false starts at getting clean, another stumble would have been the end of the line for me. The pressure was eased a little because the group was supportive, and if I did slip, it wouldn't feel like a complete failure to me since I wasn't actually in another rehab program.

It's not to say I didn't have worries. I had plenty of them. The main thing was the need to make money. A job to support myself. My musical career was in tatters, and that hurt. I may have gotten myself straight, but I still had my huge junkie ego. The necessity of a paycheck cleared that up effectively near Easter in 1996, when I took a job at a cozy little Silver Lake diner called Millie's Cafe that served up comfort food to hipsters, both local and transient, and the occasional music-business people. Millie's offered a touch of hominess complete with checkered tablecloths, hearty fare, and decent coffee. I became a busboy and a dishwasher.

It wasn't an easy transition. People I knew would walk in and I'd try to stay in the kitchen and hope they wouldn't see me. My reputation was shot with so many of my old friends. "Forrest is a fuckup," was what I imagined many of them said, and I just wanted to hide away from them. Out on the floor, as I picked up dirty plates and silverware, I'd keep my head down and clear the tables as fast as I could so I could get back into the safe anonymity of the kitchen. I saw myself as "that guy who used to be somebody." And now look at me. One day, as I was elbows-deep in a pile of dirty dishes while hot water sloshed down around my shoes as I sprayed off the plates before I racked them into the washer, I heard a girlish voice behind me. "Bob? Bob Forrest?" I turned around and was confronted with the sight of a gorgeous, fit, sexy platinum blonde I immediately recognized as singer Gwen Stefani from the band No Doubt. She was luminescent. What the hell? What was she doing back here?

"I thought I recognized you. What are you doing here?" she asked.

"I work here. I'm the dishwasher. I also clear tables out front."

She looked at me, and I couldn't read her thoughts. I hoped she wasn't pitying me. That would have crushed me.

"I just wanted to stop and tell you how much I loved listening to those Thelonious Monster records. They meant so much to me. I just wanted to say thanks for all the music."

I was dumbfounded and stammered a thanks and watched her walk out. How do you respond to something like that? I also thought that maybe I didn't really give a shit anymore. Great. She liked my music. What of it? A lot of people did. Nice to know, but it didn't matter. Here, in the steamy kitchen of Millie's Cafe, I was just a guy named Bob who washed the dishes to pay the bills. I was just some former junkie who tried to live his life as best he could. I was free from dope, free from a lot of the negative feelings that had haunted me since childhood . . . and I definitely wasn't caught up in the viselike grip of the Hollywood entertainment machine. I lived day-to-day and it wasn't so bad. In fact, right then I realized that everything was okay. I might not have been a big rock star living in a mansion or driving a Bentley, but I had a roof over my head and a car. I had people who cared about me, like Anthony, Flea, and my girlfriend Max. I had a job to do and it was a beautiful spring day. I felt satisfied. I felt good. For the first time in years, I started to feel more comfortable with myself. The strangest part was that I had no idea, not a clue, why it was working this time after all my previous failures at sobriety. Sometimes, that's how recovery is.

# YOU COME AND GO
# LIKE A POP SONG

*I've decided*
*I'm not going through it again*

—"Hurt," the Bicycle Thief

n February of 1996, I got busted, got clean, and made the supplicant's journey to Cri-Help, a twelve-step facility in North Hollywood, to attend meetings and get the counseling I needed to help me stay on the straight and narrow. The music business—among other things—had left me traumatized and I knew I needed to do what so many people had told me to over the years: *Just grow up, man!* It wasn't an easy thing to do. I had very little training in it. The music business is practically designed so that the performers live in a state of perpetual adolescence. I started working at Millie's Cafe, and, for the first time in years, I went to a real job. I stayed eighteen months in that sheltering, humbling cocoon before I decided I had to move on. But there was no way I was ready to go back to the music business, even though I wasn't qualified for much else. I became reclusive and resentful, a tightly wrapped ball of self-pity who avoided old friends, at least the ones who still cared about me, simply because they had successful music careers and here I was, a dishwasher. I had also burned bridges and run scams as a dope fiend—it goes with the job description—and a lot of people didn't want anything to do with me.

I took a job as a messenger for a movie company. The streets of Hollywood were ones I knew intimately and although they were the same dirty, crowded, traffic-choked avenues they had always been, I saw them from a completely different perspective now that I was shuttling envelopes and packages from place to place. I wasn't a rock star anymore, that's for sure. I was just another anonymous Worker Joe who did the nine-to-five to pay the bills and take care of my own day-to-day expenses. It was tough work, but it was also good to be out in the open and feel the wind blow through the window as I drove down Hollywood Boulevard. The famous names written in brass and embedded in the slick terrazzo left little impression on me. The ghosts of Hollywood's past may have been all around, but to the tourists who walked up and down the street in flip-flops and T-shirts, many of those names didn't register a blip. Once you're gone, people forget who you are. It felt like it had happened to me. I had put a lot of time, energy, and work into my music career, and now I had nothing to show for it.

It was a difficult time for me, but I had my girlfriend, Max Smith. She's probably the most significant woman in my life other than the mothers of my children. I had been on the radio call-in show *Loveline* one night. She told me after we had been dating for a while that she first became of aware me when she heard me on that show. I was fucked up, for sure, but I was also funny, open, and vulnerable. She listened in and turned to her brother and said, "I'm going to marry that guy someday." We didn't get married, but we had a long and happy relationship. She was thirteen when she heard that show. She was always very supportive. I had met Max a few years before when she was nineteen and I was thirty-two. It was instant infatuation. She was a pretty, wild girl and could match me bad habit for bad habit. But she found that the party-hard life wasn't what she wanted for herself and she cleaned up. I wasn't ready for that, and she seemed to understand. While she maintained her sobriety, I did my best to stay loaded. Through it all, she stood by my side, even when I'd engage in some questionable behavior. There was a famous rock chick who fronted a well-known band who had a taste for the narcotics. But as her fame and profile increased, sometimes it was easier for her to have me do the dirty work. She'd give me cash to go make a score and off I'd go to take a generous "finder's fee" in product for myself, or, as I did more than once, use all that I had bought myself. It wasn't like she couldn't afford it.

"Bob, where's the stuff?"

I'd stammer some lame excuse and add, "But you know I'm good for it."

"You're such an asshole," she'd say with barely concealed contempt. "Now, if I give you some money, will you please go and get me a little something?"

"No problem," I'd say.

"Okay, and no fuckups this time, right?"

"No, no, it'll all be cool," I'd say, unsure as to whether I'd run yet another hustle.

But after my bust, and my subsequent release from the clutches of the penal system, Max was there for me. She helped me along in my sobriety and she understood what I was going through. She had a great deal of empathy and seemed to know what I needed even when I didn't. She gently prodded me forward. With her encouragement, I started to give some thought to music again. Music came back into my life, but in a strange sort of way.

I still played guitar, but not professionally. I'd play Dylan and Neil Young songs at home, but with no goal or purpose other than to entertain myself and Max.

"You really should start to play out again, Bob," she said one night.

"I don't know . . ." I trailed off, unsure if anyone other than my girlfriend would want to hear what I had to sing.

"Bob, you're a musician. You can't keep hiding from the world."

"I'd need songs."

"Well, write them. You're just looking for excuses to not do this."

"I'd have to start a band or get someone to jam with," I said. "It's how I work best."

"I think I know somebody," said Max. "He's really good."

That was a surprise. It was more of a surprise when I met the musician she had talked about. Josh Klinghoffer was a gangly fifteen-year-old kid in Chuck Taylor high-top sneakers. He lived around the corner from her. He was a friend of Max's brother. I thought, *What the fuck is this? He's just a kid.* Josh didn't help himself either with his demeanor. He was so quiet and shy, he could barely look me in the eye when we talked. Even when he played music, on either the drums or the guitar, he kept his head down and his spindly teenage arms and legs tucked in tight. I thought at first that maybe this kid was autistic or something. But, no, he was just a diffident youngster who had a lot of talent. We started to have little jam sessions and we played a couple of covers gigs. I began to write again and Josh and I would record demos on a little four-track tape machine I had. All the bitterness and frustration of the previous years began to pour out of me, even if I only had three songs at that point. It felt good to write again, but I still had reservations about getting back into the game. I was a messenger now. A workingman. My music days were behind me. It was probably best not to set my sights too high.

One afternoon, after I had run all over town, my thirty-five-year-old bones feeling the strain as I delivered my packages—there's a reason they're called "delivery *boys*"—I saw a car parked in the lot where the Goldenvoice offices were. A guy I knew, Paul Tollett, the president of the concert promotion outfit, now known for the famous annual Coachella Valley Music and Arts Festival, was about to get into it. I had known him from my days on the music scene and I had a decent relationship with him, unlike with so many others. At least I was pretty sure I had never burned him. I was beat and thought I'd take a rest and say hello. Who knew? Maybe I could get a job with Goldenvoice delivering messages. I thought that might be cool.

"Hey, man!" I said with a smile.

It took Paul a moment to recognize me. "Bob?"

"That's me. How are you, man?"

"Good to see you. Let's go back inside and talk in my office. It's noisy out here."

The rush-hour hum and hiss of the traffic as it funneled through the artificial canyons of urban Hollywood made conversation difficult. I was glad to go inside, where the climate was controlled and cool, and I was even happier to take a few minutes to sit down in a comfortable office chair and take off a load. Paul sat across from me, his arms propped on his desk as he leaned forward. "So what's up with Bob Forrest these days?" he asked.

"This is it, man. Workin'."

"Working? Doing what?"

"Delivering messages and packages. You need anybody like that? It'd be cool to work for you guys."

"You're kidding me, right?"

"No."

I gave him the rundown of my recent past and watched his expression. "So you're not doing music anymore?"

"A little. Keeping things small."

"Writing?"

"I mean, I wrote a few things and I'm jamming with this kid Josh a little, but it's all pretty low-key right now."

"Bob, you can't just be delivering packages. You're a songwriter, man. You got a demo?"

"I'll bring you one."

I felt damaged and afraid. I cleared my throat and shuffled my feet and we set up another meeting, for which I brought the demo. Paul listened to what I had delivered. He had a thoughtful look on his face. "You know, I'm giving some thought to starting a record label, Bob, but I'll need artists. You'd be perfect for what I want to do. A good fit."

I thought it was cool that he didn't hold my reputation for fuckups against me, but I was worried about my finances.

"I don't know, man. A full-time music thing would leave me broke. I've got nothing left. A few bucks in a checking account is it."

"I'll put you under contract, Bob. Get some money for you. It'd be better than delivering messages all day, wouldn't it? One of my investors heard that song 'Hurt.' You know what he said?"

"No."

"He said, 'This song is *exactly* how I feel about things.' He also said, and I agree, that this is music that needs to be heard." I had a record deal.

Well, what was there to lose? I went home and felt pretty good. I was going to make another record. Back in business. This could work. On the other hand, I could work my ass off and have absolutely nothing to show for it. I had been down that road before.

I decided to call the band—Josh and I with an assist from Kevin Fitzgerald, who was from a group called the Geraldine Fibbers—the Bicycle Thief. The name came from Vittorio De Sica's 1948 movie about a man on a search for the stolen bike he needs to earn a living. De Sica's style also conveyed something of what I hoped to achieve: a gritty, unflinching realism that came out of my own experiences and feelings. Josh and I jammed and rehearsed and I began to put the songs together. Max was out one day when the phone rang.

"Hello?"

"Is Max there?"

"No. She'll be back later."

"Can I leave a message? It's Jill."

"Sure. Let me get a pencil."

Jill left her message and I wrote it down carefully on a piece of paper that I placed neatly next to the phone. Then it struck me: "I have a song here." It's weird how it works, but that incident captured how I felt as I made the journey from Old Bob to Newer Bob. In the old days, I might not have answered the phone at all. If I did, and the call wasn't for me, I'd likely have forgotten about it. Drug addiction breeds a special kind of selfishness. Since I'd cleaned up, I was gradually remembering how to be respectful and courteous. Pencil still in hand, I scribbled down some lyrics under the note "Max, Jill Called."

*The telephone is ringing*
*But it's not for me*
*Gotta remember to*
*Write a note Max Jill called*
*Gotta learn to be considerate*

Our sound was spare and raw. Acoustic-driven. Unplugged. John Frusciante, who had by now gotten clean too, came by and would add guitar parts. Songs took shape and it all began to fall into place. Paul Tollett loved what he heard. He was now in the record business and I felt good that I was the reason the Goldenvoice label came into existence. I had what I thought was a great collection of songs. They were real and they took an unflinching look at my life. "The Cereal Song" was one that was special to me. It summed up everything: drugs, addiction, and where I was at. Over the song's simple chordal structure punctuated with electric-guitar harmonics and jagged little fills, I sang about my love for heroin and cocaine.

But it wasn't rock-and-roll decadence anymore. It was regret and redemption. It was working regular, anonymous jobs and being out of the loop. It was dental problems. But I didn't want to be saccharine about it. I wanted to be truthful. My teeth, from years of neglect and drug abuse, were a mess. It's an occupational hazard. Ask Keith Richards and Shane Mac-Gowan. When I smiled, it was a horror show. And worse, I couldn't eat much more than mushy, half-liquid gruel. It was a drag, but it inspired a stanza about what drugs had given me in return for all the years of devotion I had given them:

> *Just some teeth I can't chew*
> *My favorite cereal with*

Bleak, but truthful. The song crystallized every pain and regret I felt about what I had done to myself and what I had seen happen to my friends. Where had it gotten me? I had an answer for that:

> *Thirty-five years old now*
> *I wash dishes in a restaurant*

An angular solo by John Frusciante fleshed out the sound of "The Cereal Song" and we had something that was, I thought, one of the best things I'd ever written. This album was my masterpiece, and it was released by Goldenvoice in 1999. The record got mostly positive reviews.

In October of that year, Paul Tollett launched the first Coachella Valley Music and Arts Festival. It was an ambitious project. It was a two-day event that featured five stages, all of it set up under the blazing desert sun. In that part of the world, not far from where I had lived as a kid, the brutal summer lingers on well into November. Goldenvoice brought together a lot of acts. The headliners were Beck—who not many years before had been booed off the stage at the Viper Room—Rage Against the Machine, Morrissey, and Tool. The Bicycle Thief, Goldenvoice artists, were on the undercard along with the Chemical Brothers, Jurassic 5, Perry Farrell, Gil Scott-Heron, Ben Harper, Kool Keith, and a whole bunch of other bands, DJs, and hip-hoppers. The performers all carried some serious musical credibility . . . and, unfortunately, didn't draw a huge crowd. At least not as large as we all would have expected. And although Goldenvoice had experience promoting shows, this was bigger and crazier than anything else they had done. It was great, but it was disorganized.

There were some electrifying performances that day. Beck, who had ditched his neo-folkie thing from his club days and left his leaf blower at home, presented himself as a born-again soulster who, despite looking like the whitest white boy in the whole white-boy world, managed to kick out some downright funky sounds with his band. Morrissey showed that he had some real connections to Southern California's Hispanic community when hundreds of young Latino kids—most of them boys—crowded the stage for his set. Dressed in the typical Morrissey drag of stiff and cuffed Levi's and white T-shirts, the kids also sported Morrissey's short-back-and-sides pompadour haircut and mimicked their hero's odd, arm-swinging dance moves. Perry Farrell led some kind of crazy conga line. Tool, of course, was heavy, and Rage Against the Machine pummeled the audience with its style of firebrand political rock. Josh and I turned in a good set, although Josh's shoe-gazing stage presence still struck me as goofy. "Dude, you need to connect with the audience," I'd tell him.

"But this is how I play," he'd say.

I never even knew how tall the kid was because he'd curl into himself, head down and permanently hunched over his guitar.

"They have these stools for us to sit on," I'd say at a gig.

"That's cool, man. I'll just sit on the stage floor," he'd say with a shrug.

It was maddening to me. In a festival setting like Coachella, you need to command an audience's attention. And you're not going to do that if you refuse to even look at the crowd. The stage is not the same as your bedroom.

Coachella was a huge undertaking. It had very little of the military precision that the festival features now. There were some problems with money. A lot of the bands agreed to be owed their performance fees. We were all friends, so it seemed uncool to blow that over money. But not everyone on the ticket took that attitude. Rage Against the Machine, which had fostered its image as a group of radical, fight-the-power communists, was adamant that they be paid. The money troubles led to the dissolution of the Goldenvoice label.

I was a free agent once again. The record had done well, though. It had gotten a lot of critical praise and sold steadily, but I needed distribution. Danny Goldberg of Artemis Records, a man who had managed Kurt Cobain, had listened to the record and he loved what he heard. I was at home when the call came. I let the answering machine take it. "Bob? This is Irene from Danny Goldberg's office. Could you please get back to us?"

I listened to the message. The whole idea of the music business still seemed distasteful to me. The guys at Goldenvoice were friends, so it was low-key and I trusted them. Goldberg was a different sort of creature. He continued to call. Eventually, my resistance weakened and we finally talked. I was curious.

"Bob, you've been hard to reach."

"I'm scared," I told him truthfully.

"Look," he said, "why don't we sit down and talk? I really think we can do something with your record. I listened to it and I loved it."

He "loved" it? Well, if there's one way to get through to me, it's via praise and flattery. I'm no different in that regard than most people. I thought to myself, *Well, what can it hurt to just meet with the guy to see what he has to say?*

"Okay," I said. "I can manage that."

"Good, good," he crooned through the phone. "Why don't we meet at the Four Seasons hotel over on Doheny?"

"Sounds great."

"Tuesday at eight o'clock?" he asked.

"I'll see you then," I said, and put down the phone.

I got ahold of Josh. "Look, man, we have a meeting with Danny Goldberg. All I'm asking is two things. Let me do the talking and please at least make eye contact with the guy and shake his hand. You know, be polite."

"God, Bob, I know how to behave with people."

The Four Seasons is the typical entertainment-biz place to

eat and meet. Lots of greenery around that sets up a vibe that says although you're smack in the middle of one of the busiest corridors of the city, you're miles away from it all. The ground-floor lounge is casual in that kind of way that people with money have: elegant but low-key. Danny was already seated when Josh and I arrived. I introduced them and Josh shook his hand, made eye contact, and then folded into himself like always and stared at his menu while Danny and I talked.

"Bob, the record's great, and I know we can package it and sell it." He listed all the advantages Artemis could bring to the party and I sat and listened. It sounded good. I was polite and Danny didn't have a trace of the hostility or distrust toward me that I had expected. In fact, he was very charming. We ate and talked and by the end of the meal, we had come to a deal. I felt good about it.

On the way home in the car, Josh was quiet. I could sense that something was up with him. "What?" I asked after the third mile had passed without his saying a word.

"You trust that guy?" he asked me.

"Yeah. This is a good deal. Why?"

"I don't like him," he said. "He seems slippery."

"Well, you don't know much about it, do you? That's how all these guys are."

"I still don't trust him at all, man," he said, and then went back to silence.

Well, he was a kid. What did I expect? He'd get over it, I thought. Besides, it was my band. But the seed of suspicion had been sown, or maybe it was just Josh growing up and coming into his own as a musician. We started to feud over trivial things, and I have never been good when it comes time to face criticism. These were my songs. I'd written them. I didn't need outside input. Besides, the record sold steadily. I had obviously done something right, but I had also discovered through Paul Tollett that Danny Goldberg's first reaction when he had heard I was back making music was "Bob Forrest? Are you fucking kidding me? Fuck that guy! I wouldn't touch him in a million years. He's trouble. Worthless."

What changed his mind? Tollett told me it was all thanks to a Hollywood actress. Rosanna Arquette, another one of that crowd who loved the music scene and musicians—she had a long-term relationship with Toto keyboardist Steve Porcaro and was friends with a lot of music-biz people—knew about what had happened with Goldenvoice through her friendship with Paul. She liked the record and kept talking it up to Goldberg. She had been relentless, and eventually, Danny gave me a fair shot. Never underestimate the persuasive powers of a pretty woman.

But the constant arguments with Josh started to wear me down. My own words seemed to come back to haunt me.

*I've made my bed now*
*I'm gonna lay in it*
—"Hurt," the Bicycle Thief

Another one of my bands had just taken its first step toward a premature end.

# THE EDUCATION OF BOB FORREST

A hard lesson I've learned over the years is that I don't always work well with others. Ask anyone who's ever worked with me. Especially in the music business. It's a tough gig and it plays with your mind. It can also do strange things to your ego. From the time I was a kid, I always thought that I was right about everything. Maybe it sprang from being spoiled and indulged as a child. Maybe I was just a born egomaniac. The Bicycle Thief had blown up and was "on hiatus." I broke up with Max. It was a repeat from the Thelonious Monster days: I was a difficult asshole. During my doper days, I could blame my behavior on an addict's typical selfishness, but sober, I had to face facts and try to work at humility a little harder. However, in my defense, when I write songs based on my life and my view of the world, I put myself out there on display. If someone doesn't like it, it's as if they've said they don't like me. It's a painful thing when that happens—it stings—and I react poorly. I react way out of proportion. It doesn't always lead to harmony or long-lasting musical partnerships, but as a song-writer, I've never really been anybody's partner.

So, on the one hand, I didn't have a band anymore and I was angry and frustrated. On the other hand, I had made a consid-erable amount of money from the Bicycle Thief and didn't have the immediate need to get back to work as a dishwasher or a messenger, the two jobs that had kept me grounded before my second ride on the music business merry-go-round. So what did I do? I sat in my house and did nothing. I pouted. I watched a lot of television. I ordered take-out food. I stopped attending recovery groups. I shut down communication with my friends and hid from the world to an even greater degree than I had when I took the dishwasher job at Millie's Cafe. I could see a pattern developing, but I didn't do anything about it. I just stayed inside like I was Norma Desmond from the movie *Sunset Boulevard*. Anthony Kiedis came by to offer some blunt wisdom.

"I don't know if I like this new Bob," he said as he studied me like I was some new species of virus under his high-powered mental microscope.

"What are you talking about?" I asked, and tried to sound outraged even though I pretty much knew where he would go with this.

"You were a much better person when you were just a regu-lar guy," he said. That stunned me like a slap to the face. "You worked and you helped people. Now . . ." He looked around at the place I refused to leave.

He was right. I was aimless here and it didn't serve me at all.

"What should I do?" I asked. I felt helpless. Lost.

"I don't know, man, but you need to do something. You're miserable like this. You have no purpose."

He was right, but I didn't want to believe him. I stayed home, but Anthony wouldn't let it go. He kept after me for weeks. "Why don't you go to MAP?" he said. MAP was the Musicians Assistance Program, a junkie collective where addicts helped other addicts. John Frusciante had gone there and it had helped him to clean up, something I would have thought impossible back in the early nineties, but now, when I'd run into him, he looked at the world through clear eyes. Oh, he was still John, but he wasn't Junkie John anymore.

"What am I going to do there?" I asked.

"See if they need anybody to help out around there."

It hit me: *That's actually a really good idea. Anthony's a really smart dude sometimes.*

It had always made me feel good to help people. And kindness and a supportive hand offered to others are always good things to extend in this world, so I always tried—even when I was practically incapable—to assist where I could, although it could be a cruel and devastating thing when my advice was refused or ignored and something bad happened. Rob Ritter, a gander-necked wraith with a Tennessee waterfall of a rockabilly pompadour, was a great friend of mine who played bass for a time with Thelonious Monster under his stage name Rob Graves. He also was a serious and reckless fellow traveler on the drug path. While I didn't set the best example in those years, I tried repeatedly to get him to cool the more destructive elements of his habit, but with little success. "Jesus, Bob. You're not my fucking mother . . . and you're probably the last person who should be giving me advice about dope, man," he'd say with an annoyed look on his face. When he overdosed and died in 1990, it was a terrible blow. But I learned that while I could offer help and point people in the right direction, it didn't always work. I also knew that some people were receptive to my advice and that I could help them. I just had to figure out a way to do that.

I went to MAP like Anthony suggested . . . and met one of the most significant people of the second act of my life. Buddy Arnold, the program's director and founder, was a crusty, cantankerous old guy. He was also a kind and understanding one. MAP was strictly an outpatient thing, and Buddy and I hit it off right away. Like me, he was a musician and a guy who knew everybody. A former jazz sax player, Buddy was a shiny-skulled, smiling hipster who had worked with people like Tommy Dorsey, Buddy Rich, Stan Kenton, Tex Beneke, and Neal Hefti—the man who wrote the memorable theme music for TV's *Batman* series. He knew everybody from that scene, from Billie Holiday to Stan Getz and every jazz-cat heavyweight in between. Buddy had derailed his own career with a nasty and debilitating narcotics habit and had done prison time as a result of his addiction. We were very much alike. Although we were separated by wide gulfs of time, the cultural touchstones of our respective generations, and vastly different musical idioms, we were two sides of the same well-tossed coin. He became a father figure to me. Buddy was great. He didn't preach to me. In fact, he didn't really tell me much of anything. Mostly, he provided me little hints and glimpses of what a life without drugs could be. I admired the way he walked through life. He seemed to have few regrets and was completely comfortable with himself. He didn't worry about being cool. He just kept on keeping on. I wanted what he had and I began to spend a lot of time with him. He recognized something in me too and took me under his wing. I slowly started to learn the ropes of recovery. Buddy was my mentor. He taught me how to run a group. He showed me how the industry works and how to negotiate its twists and turns. He could be tough. I went with him once to Pasadena Recovery Center to look for beds for some clients who needed inpatient care. Rehab places, like anything else in the world, hate a vacuum, and if there are empty beds, they lose money. Buddy was well aware of this, and he had also been around the block enough times to know how to play the game.

"I need some beds," he said in his gravelly rasp.

The rehab center's director blinked, gulped, and quoted him a rate.

Buddy exploded. "Are you crazy? That's too much. There's no way these folks can afford that."

"Buddy," he said, already defeated, "you know how this works."

"You're right. I do. You have empty beds and you're not making a cent off them. I can fill them by tonight." He wrote down a number on a piece of paper and slid it across the desk.

The director looked at it and took a beat. He sighed. "Buddy—"

"I don't want to hear it," he said. "Do we have a deal?"

There was no further point in discussion. Argument and resistance were futile. Buddy was a powerful life force. "Yes, Buddy, we have a deal. Bring your clients over."

As we walked out into the sunshine, Buddy smiled at me. "And that's how you do it."

I had to admit, Buddy had style and could get things done. He was comical. He could be narcissistic. He had quirks. If there was a problem, he wasn't shy about taking it straight to whoever was in charge. I saw this in action one day. Buddy had gotten word that one of his MAP clients, a famous female singer whom Buddy had sent to the Cri-Help program in North Hollywood, had gotten sexually involved with her counselor. This is considered strictly taboo for obvious reasons. I'm not saying it doesn't happen, but it can be a big deal when it does. Buddy flipped out. I went with him over to Cri-Help. He charged through the doors and made his way up the steps to the administrator's office. The receptionist went into panic mode.

"Sir! Just where do you think you're going?"

"I'm going to talk to Jack . . . your boss!" he rasped, and demanded to see the man who ran the facility.

"You can't just barge in like that!"

"Watch me," said Buddy. He had worked himself up into a towering rage. He stormed into Jack's office, while I stood there confused.

Jack was startled when the door burst open and Buddy stormed in. He tried to calm Buddy down. "Buddy, what's the problem?"

"I want to talk to that fucking counselor of yours *now*! He's sleeping with one of my clients!" Buddy was red in the face and ejected a spray of spittle with the force of his words.

Jack said, "Okay, okay. He's here now, but I think he's with a client. Let's go down the hall to his office and we can straighten everything out."

Buddy was already out the door and stomping down the corridor. He turned to me. "You wait here." I stood there like an idiot, still not exactly sure what was in play. The counselor's client was asked to wait outside for a moment. She and I stood there and looked at one another as if to say, "Oh, my God!"

Buddy slammed the door, but the conversation was heated, so we could hear everything. Buddy repeated the same question over and over: "Are you fucking that girl?"

I could hear the answer from where I stood. It was a weak answer. "I don't know what you're talking about," said the counselor.

"Are you fucking that girl?" Buddy asked again. It was like his brain was stuck.

"Uh, I don't really feel comfortable with this line of questioning," the hapless counselor said.

Jack, the counselor's boss, spoke up. "You need to answer the man's question. If you're having a sexual relationship with a MAP client, I need to know about it. Buddy and I both need to know about it."

There was a pause and I heard the counselor answer. "No. We're not. But we're . . . friendly."

Buddy's voiced became high pitched and he said, "You stay away from that girl!" Then the door burst open and I followed Buddy back down the hall to the parking lot. "He's fucking her," he said with certainty.

Turns out, Buddy was right. Once it became impossible to deny, the counselor was fired from Cri-Help. The local recovery community can be a small one and I eventually heard the whole sad story. After the counselor spent nearly a year trying to save the famous female singer, she relapsed. Because she had plenty of other problems besides addiction, complete chaos entered into the unfortunate counselor's life. Cops were called several times to break up their messy spats. He couldn't find counseling work because everybody knew what had happened. He was ostracized within twelve-step circles. A poorly chosen affair had ruined the guy, and he knew it. It was over. He gave up. He capitulated and started using drugs with the famous female singer. They partied hard and he went through all the money he had left to support their habits. He lost everything. And when there wasn't anything left to take from the poor sap, the famous female singer left him. Eventually, she pulled herself out of her addiction and got sober. The former counselor was left stigmatized here in Southern California. It was a hard, painful lesson for the both of them, but one that could have been avoided if they had only listened to Buddy, even if he did go a little bit nuts when he told the counselor to stop seeing the woman.

But I liked working with a teacher like Buddy. It struck me as very Zen. Through Buddy, I began to learn a trade. He taught me things that students in a chemical dependency school will never learn. Buddy's tutelage amounted to a Ph.D. in the business of recovery, but I didn't really know anything about the clinical side of things. It was all arcane stuff I learned from Buddy. He taught me the importance of building a team. A lot of rehab centers overlook this and it's crucial to any program's success. The standard approach to treatment for many places is monochrome. It operates from the top down. There's an owner/operator who sets up a little corporation and everybody who works there is a reflection of what the owner wants them to be. They're not allowed to be themselves. The owner is usually not involved in the day-to-day aspects of the place. Profit is often more important than a patient's recovery. Buddy had a different view. "Bob," he said, "we can't all be the same." Buddy believed that a successful program involved a staff of individuals, each with a distinct role to play. There needs to be an authority figure patients can put their trust in. There needs to be a motivational figure to prod addicts to take difficult steps when they don't want to. And there needs to be a lovable fool whom substance abusers can relate to and confide in. It's how the dynamic of a team should work, and that's what Buddy taught me. I could never have learned that in a classroom. With Buddy's guidance, I eventually worked my way up to the position of clinical director at MAP.

I knew I had chosen the right career path for myself. It was a career that had longevity. There are always going to be addicts and they're always going to need help. But I wasn't going to do it at MAP. Buddy was old and he was sick. I had seen myself as positioned to succeed him at MAP, but it became increasingly clear that wasn't going to happen. As I was told one day by one of the organization's directors, "Bob, you really don't know shit about chemical dependency. You know about treatment, but you don't know about addiction. You just know what Buddy told you. There's a whole other side to it." MAP was destined to become a very defined program once Buddy was gone and I wasn't going to be part of it. How could I? I didn't know anything about it. I couldn't speak in a director's meeting. All I knew how to do was to be me and how to put the right people together. The writing was on the wall.

In 2001, I enrolled in the chemical dependency counselor certification program at Glendale Community College. I started to come to an understanding of why my experiences with so many drug counselors had seemed so fruitless. A lot of people who enter the field are just . . . not very bright. I saw this in action one day when I made a comment during a lecture and used the phrase *ad infinitum* and inadvertently sidetracked the whole lesson when the phrase confused the class and the instructor had to stop and explain the term—which muddied up the class even more. I couldn't see myself staying for two years to acquire my certification under those circumstances, so I looked into fast-tracking. Fortunately, Crescent College in nearby Huntington Park offered a course as part of its practical nursing program. It would only take seven months. It was a better choice, so I went for it and was certified by the state of California later in the year.

I didn't learn as much as I should have. Pupils only receive a limited education in a classroom setting. I continued my fieldwork, but the course work came fast and hard and a lot of the technical stuff seemed like gibberish to me. I did what I had in high school: I listened to what the instructor discussed and tried to absorb as much as I could. I already knew the psychology of chemical dependency because I had lived it, but that was intuitive. The clinical terminology was all new to me. No matter how frustrating and difficult the class work was, I knew that once I got certified, I would be set. People already knew me from MAP and from Pasadena Recovery Center, where I also worked. I was seen as a "personality." Potential employers didn't care about me. They wanted to hire the image they called "Bob." It was kind of weird. I was good at what I did, but not everybody wanted to look deeper than the surface.

Around this time, I reconnected with Dr. Drew Pinsky in the parking lot at Pasadena Recovery Center. We had a history.

I was acquainted with him before he became a well-known specialist in the treatment of addiction. When I first met him, he was on a Saturday-night radio call-in show in the 1980s called *Loveline* that broadcast from Pasadena's KROQ-FM. I was still with Thelonious Monster back then. Drew had just completed his M.D. at the University of Southern California and was doing his residency. He hosted the medical segment of the show, during which he offered clinical advice about sex and relationships. The show would have guests, and because I was "that kid who knew everybody," I might show up with whoever had been scheduled to appear, or I'd just pop in on my own. It was fun to be on the radio. I thought I was charming most of the time, but I also showed up drunk, high, and incoherent a lot too. I disrupted the show on-air sometimes by walking off so I could go outside to do drugs. So much so that the show's producer confronted me one night.

"Look, Bob, we need to talk."

"The show tonight was great, wasn't it?" I said enthusiastically, jacked on the twelfth hit of crack I'd had over the past hour. It was a cold night and I was wrapped in an overcoat that had somehow grown several sizes too large for me. I pulled a pint bottle from one of the pockets and took a slug of vodka.

"No. The show sucked. It was terrible because of you."

I stood there shocked. I thought I had been the best part of the night's entertainment.

"You didn't even make sense," the exasperated producer said. "And I know why you kept leaving. I mean, have you taken a look at yourself lately? Drew thinks you have fuckin' AIDS, man."

I started to argue but was cut off. "Man—"

"So until you get yourself un-fucked and get your shit together, we don't want or need you here."

And that was that. It hurt my feelings, but I didn't need the show. It's not like they paid me or anything. Fine. Whatever. I stomped out and didn't return. So much for my charming personality.

In 1997 or 1998, Bill Nye "the Science Guy" from TV organized a lecture with MAP for a series he was doing on addiction. It was at the Sheraton Universal in Universal City and I went to listen. I plopped down in the front row. Nye did his thing and then brought out a guest to speak about treatment methods. It was Drew. He lectured the crowd of about twenty people in his earnest manner and then opened things up for questions. I had a few.

"Can a nonaddict ever truly reach an addict?"

"Why is the recovery rate for traditional treatment programs so abysmally low?"

Drew answered all my questions, but I had the distinct impression that he didn't remember me. How could that be? I had done all those radio appearances with him. When the lecture was over, I approached him.

"How've you been, Drew?" I asked.

"Good, good. You sure ask a lot of questions. Have we met?"

"Drew, it's me. Bob Forrest. You don't remember me?"

A look of surprise washed over his face. He looked like a man who had just seen a ghost. Little did I know . . .

"Bob Forrest? I thought you were dead."

"Come on, Drew. The hat. The glasses. Who else would it be?"

"I thought it was just . . . Holy crap, Bob, you look great!

I mean, I've seen the transitions that addicts can make, but I'm looking at a miracle."

"Look, I know you're at Las Encinas. I wonder if there's any work available for me over there."

"Did you go to school, Bob?" he asked me.

"Yeah, but I did a fast-track program," I said as honestly as I could. "But I've done lots of fieldwork."

He must have seen something in me, because he invited me to interview at Las Encinas. I showed up the next week and Drew laid it out for me.

"Bob, what you're doing now is beyond your expertise and training. I can bring you along here. Consider this 'the education of Bob Forrest.' I'll make you an administrator. You're going to learn how sick people work, and if you stick with it and give it all you've got—and read the books—you'll end up running a program."

I was scared to death when I went to work with Drew because I knew that I didn't know enough. More important, Drew knew it too. I couldn't fake it and I was unprepared. When it came to the clinical stuff, the medical and the psychological jargon, I was lost. Drew encouraged me. "If you don't know something, Bob, ask," he'd say. When we'd have staff meetings and people talked in an alphabet soup of acronyms and clinical terms, Drew said, "Get a medical dictionary and highlight pen. Look up words you don't understand. There's a lot that happens in these meetings and you won't get any of it if you can't understand what we say." It was a learning process that took years.

But I was good with patients. I could keep addicts in a program even when they wanted to bolt. I calmed the friction that sometimes blew people out of rehab.

"Bob, this place sucks. I can't take it here."

"What's the problem?"

It could be almost anything. "They don't treat me right. They talk down to me. They're late with my medication. They told me I couldn't smoke over in that area."

"Well, look. I can see your point, but come on. Those are the reasons why you want to leave? You want to leave because you want to get high. And if you leave now, you'll be high within twenty-four hours. Guaranteed."

The thing that I've found is that addicts have an almost unwavering belief in the righteousness of their arguments and complaints. About everything. And a lot of the time, they are right. I'll take their side against the facility. But my job is to get them to see that the real issue at play isn't some supposed slight or a restriction, but that those are just excuses to give in to the disease. If you throw bullshit at a patient, they'll leave. If you show some compassion and they can see that you're straight with them, most of the time, they'll stay.

I also learned that there was an underlying problem with addiction: personality disorder. It often leads to self-medicating, which often leads to addiction. And unless a person's sober, they can't begin to work on that successfully. I knew that from my own experiences. I started to see connections between my work and my personal history, although it took me a while to recognize them. When I was at Las Encinas, they'd send me to the locked ward to do consultations. I'd go and evaluate the patient.

"What do you think, Bob?" Drew would ask.

"That girl's just another addict! She could be any one of us."

"Bob, there are other psychiatric conditions besides addiction, and you have to sort those things out."

"No, no. She's been completely adulterated by medications. She's an addict and needs recovery."

"Bob, it's a little more complicated than that."

However, he did respect my belief that for a lot of patients, medicine was overdone and overprescribed. Drug addicts used to populate the fringes of society, and they slipped in and out of a shadowy world most people didn't even know existed, or, if they did, they didn't know where to find it. Now you see great, wonderful people—young, old, in between—from all walks of life who desperately scuttle about to maintain that buzz, and in the process, sometimes they overdose and die. It's a shameful thing and it gets worse every year. An entire industry keeps people doped and drugged and reaps huge profits under the guise of modern medicine.

And growing right alongside the pharmaceutical industry is the business of rehabilitation. My experiences through more than twenty different rehab programs have given me more than a little bit of insight into the game. Far too often, rehab just sells a commodity—sobriety—in the same sleazy, cynical way a late-night TV pitchman hawks used cars. And, like those cars, sobriety's often a shoddy product. What else would you call something with such a spectacular failure rate? A lot of the time it looks like a straight con job. A distraught parent or relative calls up to say, "I have a loved one who's an addict! I don't know what to do!" The calm voice on the line says, "You have to get them into treatment immediately. If you don't, *they'll die.* We have a bed waiting." Now, that's a heavy thing to lay on a near-hysterical person. When a thirty-day stay can cost tens of thousands of dollars—or more—and insurance won't cover it, then what? Well, your understanding friend on the end of the line will just transfer you over to the facility's very own credit bureau, which will advise you about mortgaging your home to pay for treatment—which may or may not do your loved one any good at all. But those beds have to stay occupied and the facility gets its cut whether the program succeeds or not. I frequently find myself questioning the ethics of this business.

People in the rehab industry want to make money just like everybody else who works for a paycheck, but too often they get greedy. I've never been overly concerned about how much money I could make at this. I want to get paid too. This is, after all, a job I do. But I don't feel the need to make millions of dollars. And if you think I couldn't make that kind of money in this industry now, you're nuts. I just couldn't live with myself if what I did was con families out of a huge fee and exploit their fear and desperation.

At times, it seems that much of the recovery industry is riddled with corruption. You can't trust anybody. Celebrities, especially, have it tough when they seek treatment. Not only are they ridiculed in the press and popular culture, they're often exploited and their confidentiality as patients is violated. Any program that treats an A-list star can get put on the map by that one famous client. One of the reasons I chose Hazelden as my first rehab facility was because Elizabeth Taylor had gone there. Some of these places are prepared to leak that information to the press, although it doesn't always happen that directly. Some hospitals have publicity and advertising departments that exist solely for the purpose of exploiting this kind of information. Worse, staff and patients have been known to sell out their celebrity clients to the tabloid press in order to flip a quick buck. Aerosmith front man Steven Tyler once told me he had been in the Priory—a well-known, high-end London clinic—for treatment and his roommate had sold the intimate details of Steven's stay to one of the big British tabloids—which all too happily published the salaciously edited details.

Almost worse is that in the effort to keep celebrity patients in the facility and to exploit them as powerful marketing tools, the stars are allowed to get away with the most outrageous kinds of behavior—things that would get a civilian patient bounced to the curb immediately. It took me several stays in different facilities to begin to learn how to game the system, but a big star doesn't have to do that. By the end of the first day they know their status and money can get them special treatment. Sometimes, they can figure that out before they even arrive.

I've heard outrageous stories, and I know they're true. Some rehab facilities—the kind that dispense daily back rubs and keep their celebrity patients on a "replacement drug" treatment—will allow their famous clients to dictate the terms under which they'll stay. One well-known pop singer once rented all the beds in an entire wing of a certain Southern California beachside center just so she could be by herself. What kind of place would allow that? That's not how we do it. It doesn't matter who you are. Here at Pasadena Recovery Center, you have a roommate. We know what works. We know how to treat drug addiction and the patients don't. We realize that as a well-off, world-famous entertainer, these people haven't had to have a roommate for many years—if ever—but it's part of the process here. Now, I won't say that we don't make certain accommodations and allowances. When you have a celebrity in treatment it changes the dynamic of the relationship with the other patients. You have to address it. You can't ignore the fact that news helicopters are flying overhead and there are roving packs of paparazzi circling the streets and climbing the trees on the perimeter. That has to be dealt with for everybody's sake.

In 2010, I felt that I could do more good operating an outpatient program, so I started Hollywood Recovery Services from the 1924-vintage, twelve-story Taft Building at Hollywood and Vine. I patterned the setup after Buddy Arnold's Musicians Assistance Program, which helped me so much. Since it was an outpatient facility, we didn't have to worry about keeping "heads on beds" and we avoided a lot of the business headaches I tend to associate with the "recovery industry." However, it was a business, and like all startups, it would take a while to see a profit. I took on a financial backer.

Maybe I should have been a little more discerning. My backer was a longtime heavyweight in the Los Angeles pornography industry who had found salvation for himself and some of his immediate family through recovery meetings. He was a gung-ho devotee of the philosophy and he liked my idea to start a program. He also liked that we had a track record through the television show, which I'll tell you all about in the next chapter. We had worked with some notoriously difficult cases in front of the cameras that had caught his eye. In particular, the actor Jeff Conaway. His appearance on *Celebrity Rehab with Dr. Drew* was tragic. He was belligerent and half-crippled, a sad, lost soul a million miles removed from Kenickie, the singing, dancing golden-boy hood he had played in the movie *Grease*. He was an addict and had been for a long time. His attempts to clean up had failed and when he checked in, he was close to total collapse from the previous night's coke-and-whiskey binge and practically an invalid from a long-term back injury. It was painful to see any human in this condition and so desperate and in need of help, but, even so, he had a fighter's spirit and a junkie's fatalism. His outbursts made audiences tune in and our backer saw how hard Drew, Shelly Sprague, and I had worked to help him. Our team had a certain marquee value that appealed to our benefactor. Unfortunately, he came from an industry accustomed to quick profits that far exceeded the investment costs. It also didn't help that Porn Incorporated was caught in an epic tailspin brought on by the Great Recession and the proliferation of freely available smut on the Internet. We folded in 2012. When the call came to inform me that our sponsor was ending our partnership, he didn't even have the decency to make it himself. He had an underling do it.

"Bob? There's going to be no more funding."

"What?"

"We're going to need you to clear out the suite and turn in your keys. We're also going to need you to give back the car we leased for you."

There was no point in arguing. It was over. "Okay, I'll have it all wrapped up by the end of the month."

"Oh, no. That won't work. We'll need you out and the car back in five days."

And that was that. We closed up shop. Porn barons are profit-driven. Extremely so. It was a noble experiment and it could have worked given time to grow. Two years just wasn't long enough. I like to think we could have made a difference, but addiction treatment is a tricky thing. No one, and I mean *no one,* is ever going to successfully beat the monster that is a drug or alcohol habit until they want sobriety for themselves. I can lead, I can show the way, but if they're not ready for what I have to offer, I advise them to stay away until they are. Do you want to know the real secret to sobriety that I've learned after all these years of rough-and-tumble personal experience? The main one is this: Don't drink and don't take drugs. You can mainline that as the straight dope.

# SHOWTIME

I n February of 2007, I had spent a long day at Las Encinas counseling my clients. Twelve straight hours dealing with the pain and frustration of addiction. Beyond that, they'd suffered additional traumas. Childhood violence, sexual abuse, personality disorders. I had listened to this litany of hurts and had tried to maintain my professional distance, but these were real people and I was affected by their stories. One kid in particular had gotten to me, an eighteen-year-old stoner with a harrowing history. A product of alcoholic parents, he had spent most of his teens numbing himself with whatever substances he could get his hands on. He had recently graduated to OxyContin that he bought on the streets for $20 per ten milligrams. His home life had been a wreck given that his father's favorite form of recreation wasn't golf or bowling but long sessions dedicated to the development of a wicked left jab. He didn't need a heavy bag. He had a son.

The kid had an acute sense of self-awareness. "I know I'm a mess, Bob," he said. "And I don't know what to do about it."

"Getting high won't help that," I said.

"It's the only thing I'm good at," he said, and it was heart-breaking.

I was still thinking about him when I arrived home. He needed rehabilitation and he was at the right place. I hoped he would stay and complete the work, but I wasn't sure. I felt a sense of relief when the key to my front door slid into the lock. I just wanted to unwind and catch my breath. I tossed my keys on the coffee table and turned on the television. I flopped down on the couch just in time to catch Jay Leno as he delivered his monologue. All the news of the day, told in Leno's nasal whine and given the humor treatment, only it didn't make me laugh. It made me angry. Rehab, addicts, and troubled celebrities were fertile territory for the funnyman, and it was a trend I had started to see filter into the popular culture. Rehab and recovery had become jokes.

Celebrities and their troubled relationships with the bottle and drugs had long been fodder for the supermarket tabloids. Actors like Robert Downey Jr., Drew Barrymore, and Shannen Doherty and their doped or drunken public antics provided splashy, breathless front-page stories for outlets like the *National Enquirer*. These kinds of stories gained even more traction with the advent of the Internet and its countless sites devoted to celebrity gossip. Just look at what happened with Britney Spears. She had, for nearly a decade, been America's pop princess, and she had come a long way from her days on Disney's rebooted version of *The Mickey Mouse Club*. After she broke through to the pop market and cemented her image as a teenage entertainer who walked the razor edge between sultry and innocent, she was constantly in the public eye. To get where she was—and it makes no difference whether you like her music or not—she had put in a lot of hard work. But in February of 2007, some major cracks started to show through her carefully crafted public persona. She checked in to—and then almost immediately out of—a drug-rehabilitation center on the island of Antigua, and now, back home in Los Angeles, she had been followed by the paparazzi vampire squad and caught in a very public meltdown. She walked into a Tarzana, California, hair salon and grabbed a pair of clippers and gave herself a number-0 buzz cut that was a throwback to Sinead O'Connor's. Following that, she attacked a photographer's SUV with a large umbrella. She checked into Promises Malibu treatment center, a sort of posh country club for celebrities in recovery. Again, she didn't stay long. Everything she did was captured on film and written about. And, given the nature of the Internet and the gossip press's hunger for celebrity scandal, she became an overnight laughingstock. Britney's troubles peaked when she was eventually taken out of her home on a stretcher and carted off in an ambulance for another rehab stint while news copters whirled overhead and photographers on the ground snapped pictures. And there was Leno, who got a big laugh when he said, "Apparently, Guantánamo Bay has the same success rate as the Promises rehab center in Malibu."

The work we all did at Las Encinas was trivialized by the media and the glare of celebrity. I talked to Drew about Leno's show the next day. "This is bullshit, Drew!" I said. "We really

201

should do a TV show about what we actually do here." Drew was in agreement.

About a year earlier at Las Encinas, I had met a dapper TV producer who liked to wear sweaters and ties. Very avuncular and personable. His name was Damian Sullivan. He was there to visit someone close to him who was in treatment. The rehab world was alien to him. I sensed he didn't know what to make of it, so I started to talk to him. I think he must have had the same perception of rehab that everybody else did: It was a joke. One hundred percent pure snake oil. I started to tell him the true story of what happens behind the walls of Las Encinas. There's real work that goes on there, and peoples' lives can be profoundly changed. I continued to see Damien when he'd visit and every time we talked, I brought up the idea of a doing a TV show at Las Encinas. Damian started to get interested and eventually thought that maybe a show about rehab would be worth doing. It wasn't an easy sell. Damian took it to fifteen different networks and they all said, "No way."

And then Britney's public meltdown happened.

I laugh now when I talk to Damian. "We owe everything to Britney Spears," I say. Once she was wheeled out of her house, the networks were suddenly interested. Celebrities admitted into rehab were hot news and VH1 jumped at the chance to do a show.

The idea we had was to show that when it came to treatment, celebrities were no different from anyone else despite what the media might portray. We pushed for doing a show that mixed celebrities with everyday people. VH1 thought about that for about two seconds before they said, "No."

Damian and I started to push and pull to shape this thing.

It had never been done. The lifted veil that would show what went on in a rehab facility required a deft hand to avoid the usual schlock aspects of reality television. After all, we'd show people's most intimate, vulnerable, and private moments, unvarnished and untreated. We also had to make sure we had the right cast assembled. Some people are better on television than others, and Damian and I had to find people who could do their jobs and who could also work effectively under the ever-open eye of the cameras. Drew, of course, was a given, but the quest to put together a team would take some thought. One of the first people who came to mind for me was Shelly Sprague, who would be our resident technician.

I had been acquainted with her since the late eighties. She ran with the same crowd and had the same bad habits as I did back in those days. I had always admired her. No matter what she did to herself, no matter what kind of trauma or abuse she heaped upon her head, she managed to hold it together. She always had a decent place to live and did okay as a hairdresser. She was also a hard-ass, and that kind of no-nonsense attitude would be crucial for this gig. I spent a lot of years as an entertainer, so I knew instinctively what would work on a show like this. When I walk onstage, I know what to do. I don't get flustered. I sensed Shelly was right for this gig. And I knew she was in the market for a job. I approached her.

"Hey, Shelly. How do you feel about reality TV?"

"I hate it, Bob."

"What would you say if I offered you a job, but you'd also have to be on this show?"

"Is this one of those 'either-or' things?"

"Pretty much."

"So what does that even mean, Bob? If I don't do the show, I don't get the job?"

"Well . . . yes."

Fortunately, she came on board. For the celebrity patients, we looked to people we knew and had treated before. This is Los Angeles, and, as the tabloid media had already shown, there was no shortage of entertainers with dependency problems. However, the network had its own ideas about who was suitable. That first season, Steven Adler, the former drummer from Guns N' Roses, was ready to go.

"Steven Adler would be great on this show!" I said. I pushed for him, but the network absolutely didn't want him. No reason given, although I suspected it may have been an image problem. Steven suffered from a nasty drug dependency that he had battled since his days with Guns N' Roses. He had suffered a stroke that was likely a result of all the abuse he had given his body during the height of his rock star fame. As a result he was left with an unsteady gait and a noticeable speech impediment. He could be difficult to understand because of it. Perhaps that was why the network was so dead set against having him on the show. When the second season came around, Steven still had problems with substance abuse and I brought him up again. This time the network was happy to have him aboard. It was crazy how it all worked. Unpredictable.

Through the grapevine, I heard that Valkyrie-like actress Brigitte Nielsen was at Cri-Help in North Hollywood. "Has anybody called her?" I asked. "I think she'd be a good candidate." A producer from the show reached her at the center and told her about what we planned to do. She agreed right away. It's pretty much how we found everybody for the show. We asked and they came . . . with network approval, of course. After that first season, after we had a hit, it became easier to find patients, but before the show made its debut, I started to get a little nervous that VH1 might not have the same goals as the rest of us. I worried that we would all look unprofessional, but I was also sure that wouldn't be in the channel's best interest. This show had the potential to do well for them, although in the back of my mind, I knew that something new like this would have no middle ground. Viewers would either love it or hate it.

Now, all this may seem a bit disingenuous coming from a guy who is best known these days as "that guy with the hat" on a reality TV series. I have had some real issues with some of the show's direction. The producers shot an entire documentary about *Jackass* star Steve-O's recovery with Dr. Drew. Steve-O, a limber, jocular guy who'd made an implausibly successful career out of performing ridiculous and dangerous stunts that generally involved his scrotum and a staple gun, had been a life-long stoner and was engaged in a serious downhill run when he came to us. Drugs were only a part of his problem. He was also addicted to the camera. While he was supposed to be going through the program and the sober house follow-up, he was shooting segments in his room with his *Jackass* costars and his producer Jeff Tremaine. It was unbelievable. He's managed to maintain his sobriety, but it couldn't have been easy with all that entertainment nonsense going on around him. I have difficulty with that Hollywood, glitzy, exploitative aspect of the show. One thing I learned fast: Television is a ruthless, heartless business. It's one with no friendships and few alliances, and it feeds and fuels itself on two items: money and bullshit. Take it too seriously and get too deeply enmeshed in the day-to-day, and it will make you crazy. Drug dealers have more ethics than television network executives, but I figured out a way to make the intrinsic greed work for me: I cut a deal. No agents, no lawyers. Just me.

I spoke with the executive producer of the show, John Irwin.

"Look, I think this show will do well and we'll do a number of seasons with it. Start me out at two thousand dollars a week, and if we're a hit, double that for the next season . . . and we'll just progress from there."

"How long do you think this show will run, Bob?"

"Five or ten years, easy. Besides, I'm putting my career at risk even doing a show like this. And I'm coming to you straight, no lawyers or agents."

"You're nuts, but okay. Deal!"

By the time we entered the third season, the lawyers came.

We all sat down at the big table. "Well, we hear that you have some kind of deal?"

"Yep."

I had started to make pretty good money by then and the show had produced spinoffs like *Celebrity Rehab Presents Sober House* and *Sex Rehab with Dr. Drew*. I was being paid well for them too, but I also realized that come the fourth season, there was no way VH1 was even going to consider continuing with the deal that I had cut. I agreed to $5,000 a week with a 10 percent annual increase. I also specified that my contract never have any mention of or stipulations about any subsequent seasons. Television can burn you out, and I didn't want to be trapped into another season if I wanted out. Five weeks on a set can be a grind, and I needed that option.

Besides the spinoffs we've done, we decided to take a new direction this time out. The new version of the show has no celebrities at all. All of our patients are just plain folks. Unlike celebrities, who have the resources to explore various treatment programs, people of average means don't really have that option. We put out ads throughout the country on places like Craigslist.org and offered treatment to people who otherwise couldn't afford it. There was no mention of VH1, Drew, or myself. We asked applicants to send·in a short video of themselves and what their goals were. We were inundated with hundreds of responses from all over America within the first hour. Some, of course, weren't genuine. Even though the ads hadn't mentioned the television show, some of the respondents figured out what the deal was and applied as a way to get on the air and make a play for reality stardom. We had a good crew that was able to discern between those who wanted help and those who hoped to become the next Honey Boo Boo.

"Please help me!" said one wolf-eyed kid from a small town in Alabama.

"I don't know where else to turn!" cried a girl with pink hair and a nose ring.

"I won't live to see next year," stated a young mother as her kids wailed offscreen and she calmly pulled on a cigarette, the curls of smoke framing her delicate face.

It was heartbreaking. These were people who had suffered and who had been victimized by bad treatment centers, and their plight put me in a strange and frightening position. Most of the patients on this new season have an abiding and unwavering faith that Drew and I are the only people who can help them. It's the power of TV. That faith can be unnerving, because nobody can wave a magic wand and administer a cure. It takes work. Not only from Drew and me, but from the patients themselves. It's a lesson I had to learn over a period of years as I faced down my own struggles. When someone says to you, "My crappy life would be different if only you were my counselor . . . and now it's happening," it puts a lot of responsibility on your shoulders. As a counselor, I've never experienced this kind of thing. Right now, as we get started with the show, it's okay. It's the honeymoon phase of things. It's usually that way. But once the weeks start to roll by and the cameras don't back off, it could all come crashing down. The words I would hate to hear are "Fuck you, Bob. You didn't do anything. I'm going home."

But that's a possibility and I have to be steeled for it. While the show has gotten praise for its demystification of rehab and how we show that the path to redemption is navigable, there are also plenty of voices that say it's sleazy and exploitative.

In 2009, the country singer Mindy McCready signed a contract to appear on the show. She was almost a living embodiment of every tragic female country star to ever have existed: failed relationships, pills, alcohol, domestic abuse, and underneath it all, a fragile vulnerability. She could have been a parody of the country music genre, but we all loved her and the audience did too. She gave all of us a huge scare when, on camera, she suffered a seizure and collapsed. All through her time on the show, she exhibited a concern and kindness for her fellow cast members and always seemed to care more about them than she did for herself. We were happy that she seemed to have conquered her demons when the season ended. But it wasn't long before her name started to appear in the media again as her troubles once more started to consume her. In February of 2013, when news of her suicide came to light, I was heart-broken. We deal with troubled people and we try our best to help, but sometimes tragedies occur.

That's the nature of what we do. All I can do is apply what I've learned and what I know and be compassionate, give encouragement, and, most of all, be real. It's showtime now. A small army of crew people from VH1 runs about with clipboards and wireless headsets. The back end of the parking lot has been converted into an eating area by a catering company, and tables and folding chairs are set up underneath a makeshift awning that flaps in the mild breeze. Smoke curls up from a portable grill that an early-shift cook uses to prepare some kind of meat as well as chicken for lunch. In a room inside the facility, somebody has laid out breakfast: bagels, muffins, cold cereal, fresh fruit, and plenty of coffee. I stack some watermelon on my paper plate. In another room a large flat-screen television set gets the feeds from several different cameras throughout the center. The center has been converted to a film set and we're all ready for another season under the unblinking eyes of the cameras.

# TREATMENT: IT'S UP TO YOU

The morning is typical for late spring in Southern California. It's softly overcast and pleasantly cool. The warm inland temperatures of the previous afternoon have drawn in overnight moisture from the Pacific that has settled as mist in the valleys and canyons and will remain suspended there until the sun burns it off in the early afternoon. It's a weather cycle that will be repeated endlessly until the summer heat of July finally brings it to an end. I'm at the Pasadena Recovery Center and the television show is in its second week of production.

The center, on Raymond Avenue, is dead center in one of Pasadena's older neighborhoods. It's what could rightfully be called a "mixed use" area. There are several convalescent homes nearby and on the larger streets are chain supermarkets and beverage outlets like Starbucks. There's no uniformity to the residences on the smaller streets, unlike newer Southern California neighborhoods that aspire toward uniformity. Here, there are small, single-family stucco homes not much bigger than shoe boxes and some stately multistory models built in a fake Craftsman style. Directly next door to the center is a sprawling old home with a sagging front porch that sits well to the rear of a weed-choked lot. A cracked cement footpath leads in from the sidewalk and is guarded by two forlorn-looking stone Chinese lions that have begun to crumble with age and time. There are ancient trees everywhere. Gnarled pines, shady oaks, and, since this is Southern California, towering palms hold up the gray skies and provide shelter to an amazingly rich variety of mountain birds down from the foothills. A ragged symphony orchestra of scrub jays, mockingbirds, and, oddly, feral, nonnative green parrots shrieks and squawks from the shelter of the branches and fronds and carpet-bombs pedestrians and parked cars with their caustic droppings. The cracked sidewalks are stained white with the stuff.

PRC itself is a low-slung ranch-style building that blends in to these surroundings well. Its front is glass with cheery-colored inserts that wouldn't have looked out of place at a California public school during the 1960s. Near the entrance are molded concrete tables and benches made to resemble stone, and a nearby tub constructed of the same stuff and filled with sand. The smokers here use it as their communal ashtray. It's well used. Inside, the floors are made of a light-colored wood and there are pressure-molded plywood chairs that mimic the famous Eames style, all organic curves and retro-looking swoops. Hung on the walls are photographs of rugged-looking islands surrounded by gently lapping seas. In the office, a few of the workers drink coffee, chat, and answer phones. Their voices float through the corridor, where a sleepy-looking security guard sits at a table with a sign-in book. Up on the roof is a lounge area for the residents with padded chairs, chaises, and potted plants. It's a modest place. Certainly nothing too fancy, but it's pleasant and has a warm and welcoming feel to it. It's about as far as one can get from the style of some of the "high-end" oceanfront treatment centers that cater to the wealthy and resemble palatial resort hotels and spas. Whatever works, as the old adage goes. But what is effective when it comes to treatment?

From personal experience, I can attest that not a single person from my peer group—the hardest of the hard-core junkies—can ever tell anyone how they were able to get clean. There's no set formula. For a very long time, I was convinced that love was the answer. I was wrong. I loved Layne Staley. Love didn't help him.

At the turn of the millennium, I had been clean for a few years and I had started to gain a reputation as someone who could talk to addicts. More importantly, they'd listen. Layne was the charismatic front man for the Seattle-based band Alice in Chains. He also had an increasingly heavy and debilitating heroin addiction. That habit, which had at one point seemed a certification of his outsider, rock-and-roll cool, now threatened to destroy him. His skin took on the look of bleached vellum, his weight dropped below ninety pounds, and he was becoming increasingly reclusive. He had entered the end stage of the game. It's the same old story, and one that I had witnessed more than once.

But he had people who loved him and who didn't want to see him check out early. His mother, especially, was worried. Somehow, she had heard that I had helped John Frusciante, so she called me.

"Layne's in terrible shape," she said. "I heard that you and John are doing okay these days. Could you please talk to Layne? Maybe you could get John to talk to him too?"

"I'll do what I can."

How could I refuse a request like that? I was aware of how bad Layne had gotten. The press loved to write about his fall. Layne was at the top of those "death pool" lists morbid people loved to put together. I gave John a call. If anyone could relate to Layne's condition, it was Frusciante.

"Hey, man. How's it going? You doing all right?" I said.

"Yeah. I'm good. What's up?"

"I got a call from Layne Staley's mother. She's really worried about him. She says he's in terrible shape. Worse than you were, maybe. She asked me if we'd go talk to him. What do you think?"

"Talk to him about drugs?" he asked.

"Yeah. Drugs. Of course drugs."

"I'll talk to him. But if he wants to do drugs, Bob, well, he should probably just do them." It was classic Frusciante. He was the guy who stood over me once when I was in the throes of an overdose and said, "Just let it go, Bob. It'll be all right."

I thought a bit more about my decision to ask John to help out.

He continued. "I don't want to preach to anybody like you and Anthony do. Look. I don't do drugs anymore. I don't like to get high anymore. But if someone wants to do them, they should. They totally should." I was kind of surprised to hear him say that, but I also realized that John, like always, was staying true to his ideals and beliefs. He was consistent. I had to give him that, and I understood where he was coming from.

"I think he's really sick, John. We should go talk to him."

"Okay."

I called Layne's mother back. "John and I will talk to him. I don't know how much it will help."

Layne's mom said she understood. "You know, Bob," she told me, "Layne's got an odd sense of humor. I told him that John had gangrene once. He said, 'In his arm? That's terrible, Mom. John's a guitar player. He needs his hands and arms. Me? I'm just a singer. I can get by without them.' I know he was joking, but I don't like to hear stuff like that. Can you try to talk sense to him?"

"We'll talk to him," I said. I hung up the phone and wondered how much good it would do. Frusciante was probably right. You can't preach to anyone. Sometimes, you can't even point them in the right direction. A horse won't drink if it doesn't want to.

And so we went and found Layne. He didn't look good at all. His mind still worked but he was a million miles away. He played a video game while we talked.

"Hey, Layne," I said. "What's going on?"

"Nothing. I know why you're here," he said as he idly fiddled with the control.

"Your mom's worried, man. You don't look too good."

"I'm okay, though. Really." I wasn't sure what he based that on. He was adamant that he was fine. He pretended to listen. Neither John nor I could reach him. The newspapers had to have had his obituary on standby. After more fruitless talk, John and I left.

"I don't think he'll come out of this," I said.

"It's his life, man," said John.

He was right. On April 5, 2002, Layne died from what the autopsy later indicated had been a coke and heroin cocktail. He had become so reclusive that nobody knew he was gone until April 19, when the police—along with his mother and father—found him decomposing in his condo after getting a tip that there had been no activity on his bank card for the last two weeks. On the table was a stash of cocaine and a couple of crack pipes.

Of the people I tried hardest to reach—John Frusciante, Jeff Conaway, Mike Starr from Alice in Chains, Steven Adler, and Jason Davis, the voice actor and oil company heir—two are dead, two are sober, and one still gets high. I loved them all, but love, or a reasonable facsimile, is never enough to fix an addict . . . even though in the absence of drugs and alcohol, an addict will search for something to fill that void. Sex is often the easiest score.

It's why I've become quite in favor of what's called gender-specific rehab—at least for the heterosexual community. Women and men in rehab almost always have some real problems in addition to their addictions. They're what might have been called in a less-enlightened time "damaged goods." They've been sexually abused or traumatized by life and usually have some form of clinical mental illness. It's not their fault. They just happen to be people living in twenty-first-century America, and a girl's got to do what a girl's got to do, as does a guy. When you put these people in a mixed-gender group, they can cause real chaos. They know how to manipulate situations and use their sexuality to their advantage. It can be tragic to watch it unfold, but there's not much anyone can do but warn against it and hope people will be able to override their basic biological urges. Mostly, it's a lot to ask, but you have to try to get them to see the light.

"Hey, man, you need to concentrate on yourself," I might try to advise some poor lovelorn addict. "Get your own life straightened out. Now's not the time to fall in love—especially with someone who, if you don't mind my brutal honesty, is way more fucked up than you are."

"Fuck you, Bob," he might spit back. "You can't tell me what to do. You don't know how I feel. You don't know how we feel about each other!"

"You sound like a goofy, love-struck teenager, dude."

"Well, maybe you're right, man," he'll say. But a week later you'll see him furtively sharing a cigarette with his rehab girlfriend and you'll know that there are some things that are stronger than any dire words of warning you might choose to use.

Redemption from the disease of addiction is entirely possible—but it has to be done alone. And yet, addicts constantly search for love and approval, and when their expectations aren't met, they become resentful. Drugs and alcohol become their intimates. These substances may wreak havoc in users' lives, but they're constants. And they're always there.

I had plenty of resentments when I started my journey. I was upset that my musical career had not followed the course I had projected. My friends Anthony, Flea, and John Frusciante had all started out like me and became some of the biggest rock stars on the planet. Why not me? What had happened? Back in the bad old days before my sobriety, I found myself at a Los Angeles drug house. It was nothing like you see in the movies. It wasn't in a "bad" part of town. There weren't gangsters with guns. There weren't even the rusted carcasses of old appliances or automobiles propped up on concrete blocks in either the front or back yard. A gardening crew came once a week and kept things neat on the outside. It was just a typical, middle-class junkie pad with comfortable furniture, a carpet that could have used a good once-over with a vacuum cleaner, and a coffee table with half-crushed empty beer cans tossed about haphazardly and ashtrays that overflowed with old cigarette butts. All the mundane detritus of addiction as practiced by white folks. There was even, almost incongruously, a big-screen television set permanently tuned to MTV to entertain the stumblers who drifted in and out to take care of business. I was bundled up in an oversized coat to protect me from the nighttime chill outside even though I poured sweat from the crack cocaine I obsessively smoked in the corner of the room. Crack is the salted peanuts of the drug world. One taste demands another. And another after that.

There was a commotion at the front door. "Hey, what's up?" said our friendly host as he ushered in a pair of new arrivals. I barely glanced up from the glass straight shooter I held to my lips and lit another rock pushed into the opposite end. I held the medicinal-tasting smoke in my lungs and blew out a huge billow of it that expanded to the low ceiling. I felt the rush hit me, a sensation of a sudden drop in pressure while the hum of a ghost train ran through my ears. "Jesus Christ," I muttered at the intensity of it. I stared blankly at the glowing TV in front of me, unable to comprehend what this strange electronic object was for a moment. I eventually focused enough to recognize it again as this thing called "television" and see that MTV was showing the latest video from the Seattle-based band Alice in Chains. As I looked past the set, I watched as the two arrivals were ushered toward the back of the house to do a little business. I recognized them as Alice in Chains singer Layne Staley and the band's bass player Mike Starr. I looked at them and then looked at the TV. Weird. Here they were copping drugs, and on-screen, they were miming their latest hit single. It was an odd thing to see and it struck me as somehow unfair. *Everyone's passing me by,* I thought bitterly. I shoved another rock into the pipe and took another hit. *Fuck it, man.*

This was the same old resentment that I had felt after Thelonious Monster recorded *Beautiful Mess* and we went out on the road. The constant tours and endless one-night shows took a heavy toll on me, and the band was tired. We played badly, I thought, but we were still a vital live act. We were better than Candlebox or some of our Capitol Records label mates that we would tour with. I thought their shows were the equivalent of watching water freeze. They weren't very fond of us, either. The bands with whom we were billed generally resented us for the chaos we brought as part of our package. We were a hard act to follow. Most of them were scared to have us open for them. It got to the point where we'd just tour with bands that were friends of ours, like Soul Asylum and Hüsker Dü. *Beautiful Mess* didn't spawn any American singles, but one of the songs, "Body and Soul?" caught on with European audiences and was a hit over there. While the song was in rotation on European

MTV, we made a lot of appearances on the music network in Europe and here in America. But we couldn't deliver the goods in any sort of sustainable way and we fell apart.

Deep down in my core, I felt like Thelonious Monster had more talent and charisma than most of the bands on the scene, but either we'd blow it at crucial moments or people just didn't get us. It was frustrating to me. I hung on to those feelings for many years. It made my relationship with Anthony Kiedis difficult at times. We were friends, for sure, but I also harbored a lot of latent resentment toward him. How dare he get so much more successful than I did? We had shared that goddamn apartment at La Leyenda. It was hard for me to understand what it all meant and where it went wrong. It took me years of therapy to get over all that. I was damaged.

In 1994, I was broke and a lot of my friends weren't. I got a publishing check for $3,500, and I went straight to a place called Bar DeLuxe to start some serious drinking. I got drunk quick and kept the bartender busy. I was with some friends and they couldn't keep up with my pace. *Fuck 'em,* I thought. *Doesn't anybody know how to party anymore?* I felt the hot, sharp need to use the restroom. I slid off my stool and pushed my way in its direction. I was unsteady and I bumped into a ponytailed waitress. She spilled the drinks on her tray. I stood there and swayed like a weed in a summer breeze. She wasn't happy. "What the fuck's the matter with you, asshole?" she spat out. I tried to throw the old Bob Forrest charm. The waitress was immune. "Who's going to pay for these drinks?" she demanded.

It made me angry that she talked to me like that. Didn't she know who I was? "Fuck you. I have to use the toilet," I said, and brusquely pushed past her. I could hear her behind me: "You're going to take care of this, jerk."

Inside the restroom, I was alone. I locked the door and took care of business. The incident with the waitress preyed on my mind. I felt ready to explode. I looked at my reflection in the mirror and didn't like what I saw. *Why hold back?* I thought. I cocked my fist and hit my reflection solidly in its nose. The mirror cracked. I dully looked down at my hand and saw the bright blood start to seep through the jagged cuts in my knuckles. I somehow felt better. I threw another punch with the other hand and smiled at how the mirror now resembled some kind of road map. I ripped the towel dispenser off the wall and threw it at the cracked mirror and watched the shards of glass fall into the sink. I kicked the metal wall that protected the toilet and put a huge dent in it. I gave it another one and made the dent deeper. I could hear someone pound on the door and heard a voice call from the other side. It was one of my friends. It snapped me back to reality. I looked around at the all the damage I'd caused. *Aw, fuck. I'm going to jail for this,* I thought. You can knock over a waitress's tray of drinks and, at most, you'll get kicked out of the bar. You engage in wanton destruction of private property and somebody's going to call the cops. I unlocked the door and my friend slipped inside. I locked it again. He took a look at the shattered glass, the dented stall, the towel dispenser that rested in the sink, and then looked at me. "Jesus Christ, Bob. What the fuck's the matter with you?"

"I'm going to jail, man. I'm going to jail." I stood there and stared at my shoes. I felt sick.

"Look, man. Nobody's going to jail. We're going to walk

straight out of here, you're going to throw a bunch of cash on the bar to settle up, and then we're out the door and gone. Got it? You don't talk to anyone on the way out and you don't say anything to anyone. Understand?"

I was in no position to argue. The fight wasn't in me anymore. "Let's go," I said. He opened the door and we walked straight ahead to the bar. Fast, but not too fast. I flipped a couple of hundreds on the bar and we were out the door and into the night.

So how did I get from a place like that, the destructive and out-of-control void, a place where I refused to take responsibility for my actions, to a place that, most of the time, resembles a state of calm? Treatment. But what was it about treatment that eventually worked for me? I still don't know. It's not like there's one thing I can point at and say, "That! That's the magical thing that fixed me and cured me and made everything right in my life and in the world." It may work that way for some people, but I doubt it. The first big step for me came at Hazelden. When I was there they told me, "You can be sober." That opened my eyes to the possibility, although I stumbled a lot of times on my journey to where I am now. Even though I had any number of relapses, I had the desire to be clean. I'd fall, but I'd get back up.

If I have one piece of advice to give, it's this: If you really want to get sober, give up alcohol and drugs for twelve months. Stay away from them. Don't touch them. Go to meetings, but use your strength and your will to not use or drink. There are people who will tell you that you have to put all your trust in God. Really? As soon as I said, "I don't have control of this situation, God does," I would have been right back in a world of hurt. Dogma is something that I've never found helpful. The support of a group can help, but use common sense too. Groups are just like anything else in life. There are cool people and there are not-cool people. You'll have to figure out who's who. And you'll have to do that, like everything else in the process, by yourself. Nobody can save you but yourself.

If you stumble and relapse, don't give up. If you really want to live your life without drugs or alcohol, you'll hit those times when you give in and use. To fall into despair over it won't help. Stop. Again. There is an astonishing failure rate when it comes to treatment. But *failure*'s an odd term to use with a disease like alcoholism and drug addiction. It's like asking someone with type 1 diabetes, "Did your insulin cure you?" Of course not. Which brings up an interesting take on the success rates of treatment programs. Drew and I don't trust the data that's out there. We talk about it. I'll see some stats and say, "We don't seem to do a great job if these figures are accurate."

"The data just depends upon how it's measured, Bob. And it isn't culled properly when addiction is studied. Addiction is viewed like pneumonia when it's more like asthma. It's a chronic illness and the end point is screwed up."

He's right. Drew also believes the studies are usually too short. Generally, they're conducted over a period of months. You don't really see studies that follow a single group of addicts over a ten-year period. Something like that might give you some insight. Another problem is that so many of the studies that are done these days involve what's called "replacement therapy." It's a fancy term for giving addicts another drug to keep them off heroin. It used to be methadone. Now it's Suboxone. It's not really a cure for addiction.

Urine tests are unreliable too. In a clinical situation, most

addicts know when they'll be tested. They know how to manipulate that. They know how to beat the system. Urine tests are
often done on the same day, week in and week out. An addict
knows how long a drug stays in the body. Have a urine test on
Monday? Well, from Friday night until Monday morning, don't
take drugs. Instead, drink heavily to cool yourself out. Your
test will come back clean. Or you can buy clean urine from a
friend to put in the specimen bottle when you're alone in the
toilet stall. It's all part of the game in the addict lifestyle. To
depend on drug addicts to give you straight facts is not a great
strategy if you want to get to the truth. Worse, abstinence is
not always seen as a cool or sexy kind of treatment. It's hard
work for the patient and it involves drastic changes in the way
life is lived. If anyone should be held up to the "succeed or fail"
standard, it should be us, the people who run these programs.
If we do anything less than attempt to give addicts who want
treatment a decent shot at sober living—without replacement
drugs—we're the ones who fail.

But the main thing to remember is that addiction isn't a
bleak dead end. There's hope. I know an awful lot of formerly
helpless dope fiends who now live bright new lives of sobriety
and have all the good things that come along with it. Did they
stumble along the way? Sure, almost all of them. The important
thing is that there's a desire to live free from drugs. If you slip
and fall on your journey to sobriety, just start over. Don't be
defeated. As they say in twelve-step meetings, "Keep coming
back. It works if you work it." And it does.

# HAPPY #12 AND #35

*I'm happy just to be alive . . .*

I may have grown older, but I still enjoyed the things that made me smile when I was a kid. Here I stood under purpling skies as the sun set at the end of a cool and pleasant day in Los Angeles, just south of downtown. I was alone in the square in front of the glass-and-steel façade of the Staples Center on Chick Hearn Court. This wasn't here when I was a kid and I tagged along at my dad's side, amped up for a night of Lakers basketball at the Forum in Inglewood before we'd enjoy a guys' night on the town, just the two of us, over in Chinatown for a postgame meal. At a restaurant called Hop Louie's Golden Pagoda, heavily accented Chinese waiters in starched white shirts and heavy crimson vests delivered a steady stream of hot, steaming plates piled with shrimp fried rice, chow mein, and great, golden, greasy stacks of egg foo yung that swam in some sort of unidentifiable brown sauce. "Eat up, Bobby," said my dad as he downed a gin and tonic in a highball glass filled with ice. There was a large aquarium along one wall, lit with a single bulb that gave the lone lionfish that swam among the plants and rocks of this artificial reef an eerie glow. "You know, Bobby, those things are poisonous," said my dad as he pointed at the aquarium with his chopsticks.

"Do people eat them?" I asked.

"I think the Chinese do. They eat a lot of different stuff."

"Is it good?" I asked.

"Maybe. I don't know. Looks too spiky for me to ever want to try one."

"Yeah, I don't think I'd like it either. Especially if it's got poison in it," I said, going back to my plate.

One of the waiters took away an empty platter that sat on the table and said something about "armond chicken." I lifted a small, handleless cup filled with tea and took a sip right as my dad shot me a comical look in reaction to the waiter's remark. I laughed hard, and warm, heavily sugared tea erupted out of my mouth and nose. Later, after we couldn't eat another bite, a solemn waiter brought a small tray with a couple of fortune cookies. "Crack it open, Bobby. See what the future holds," said my dad. I took one of the brittle treats and snapped it in half. Inside was a little strip of paper. I pulled it out and was disappointed to see that all the writing on it was in Chinese. "I can't read this," I said. My dad motioned for a waiter.

"Could you read this for us, please?" he asked, and handed the paper to the waiter.

The waiter looked at the little strip and then said, "It say, 'You have very good-a ruck.'" My dad and I broke into gales of laughter.

Here on Chick Hearn Court, I waited for Flea and Chad Smith, the rhythm engine that powered the Red Hot Chili Peppers. I had called Flea earlier. "Hey, man, we should go catch a game."

"Let's do it tonight," he said.

"Cool. Meet me at the Magic Johnson statue," I said.

An individual might be hard to locate in the kind of crowd the Lakers draw, but it was impossible to miss the recently erected tribute to Magic Johnson. Seventeen feet tall and cast in bronze, it depicted the former Lakers point guard frozen midaction in his gold uniform and old-school shorty-shorts as he led the team on a fast break, one hand palming the ball and the other pointed down court. And so I waited for my friends as the pregame crowd grew larger and made its way inside. I reached in my pocket and fished out a piece of nicotine gum. I fumbled with the foil backing and finally managed to peel it away to get to the mint-flavored lozenge inside. Four milligrams' worth of nicotine in a chewy treat. I had managed to quit cigarettes, but I still needed regular doses of nicotine. I figured that even if I had given up all my old vices, I should hang on to at least one. So it was nicotine and caffeine. Pretty safe when I considered all the other stuff that used to pump through my veins.

"Hey, man!" I heard, and looked up. Flea and Chad made their way through the throng. I thought back to when we were much, much younger and how we had lived. In those days, I don't think any of us could have pictured ourselves creeping into middle age, when a big night on the town meant a hometown basketball game. When the game was over, we didn't go out on the town and tear it up like we did when we were kids; we went home.

I left the city and drove back to the Valley, where my wife, Sam, and our baby, Elvis, waited for me. In the car, I thought back to the first time Sam and I met. It was at Las Encinas. I was intrigued by her. It wasn't anything I could pinpoint absolutely. It was any number of things. Mostly, I just thought she was cool. She stood apart from the crowd. I started to see her at different recovery meetings, but I kept my distance. I stayed at arm's length for nearly six years. Sam was admitted to Las Encinas for a second stay as an outpatient, and I finally said to myself, "This is ridiculous. Ask the girl out." It was a bold move. Staff is definitely not supposed to do that. It's one of those rules designed to keep vulnerable people in treatment safe from predatory manipulations, but I thought to myself, *I'm not a predator. I'm not a creep. I'm just a guy who really likes this girl.* I approached Sam, who, by this time, had also shown an interest in me.

"Look, you know the rules. We're not supposed to see each other socially," I said in my most professional manner.

"But . . . ," she said, which gave me tacit permission to continue.

"Maybe we could go have some dinner and talk."

"I'd like that." She smiled.

"We could get in trouble for this, you know. Me, a lot more than you."

"Nobody's going to do anything. We'll be discreet."

On December 18, we went out on our first real date and we found that there was something there. We thought it was happiness, but these things are always tricky, especially in our particular situation. Word got out and I was betrayed by a friend. Loesha Zeviar, who has appeared as a resident technician on *Celebrity Rehab with Dr. Drew,* was a director at Las Encinas. She deduced the relationship that I had with Sam and went straight to her supervisor to spell it out. I felt hurt. I had known Loesha since she was sixteen. Our relationship covered years. She was married to my friend Flea for a time. But she was scared when she learned of my relationship with Sam. She felt like she was in over her head and so she went to her boss, a guy who had only been at the facility for four months, and trouble came hard and fast. I was called into the boss's office. You know it will be bad when the first thing said to you is, "Please, sit down."

I took a seat and watched this rookie study me. I don't think he liked me much to begin with anyway. "Bob, did you go out with one of our clients?"

It made no sense to lie about it. He already knew the story from Loesha anyway. "Yeah," I said.

"Bob, this is a serious violation of our standards."

He read me the riot act, but I kept my job. I was upset. Sam was upset. But we stayed together and after a few years as a couple and the birth of our son, Elvis, we were married in December of 2012 in beautiful Las Vegas, Nevada. I don't hold any of this against Loesha. Her job at Las Encinas was incredibly difficult and I've always thought the demands placed upon her were beyond her experience. She might have handled it differently given our history, but she made her decision. And I got a lovely wife and beautiful child in the deal.

I was thinking about them as I wheeled onto our street and pulled into the drive. I fumbled with my keys at the front door for a moment before I slid the right one into the lock and walked inside. "Honey, I'm home," I said, sounding exactly like the kind of person I never thought I could be when I was lost in my increasingly faraway wasted years. Sam and I went to look in on Elvis, who was asleep in his bed. I thought to myself, *I may not be completely well, but I'm much, much better.* And I was happy.

# ACKNOWLEDGMENTS

**Bob Forrest** wishes peace and love to Pete, Josh, Flea, Anthony, Dix, Chad, Morty, Norwood, J.D., Zander, Shelly, Drew, Sasha, Loesha, Doc Sheila, Paul T., Skip, all the girls I've loved, the ghost of Joe Strummer, Gibby, my family. . . . Everyone who is in my life, I can't thank you enough!

**Michael Albo** thanks Bob Forrest for taking me on as his "with" guy, Evan Wright for his sage advice, Richard Abate for putting this book together, Suzanne O'Neill and Anna Thompson for their guidance, Frank and Diana Albo for their support, Kari Nelson, Crystal Taylor, and Amanda Colbath—the High Priestesses of the Pour—for making sure my glass was always full, and Tristen Pelton for her kind and sympathetic ear.

# ABOUT THE AUTHORS.

Bob Forrest is "the guy with the hat" on VH1's *Celebrity Rehab with Dr. Drew*. He's a certified addiction specialist and counselor as well as a musician. A rock-and-roll Zelig who has been on the Los Angeles music scene since the early eighties with his bands Thelonious Monster and the Bicycle Thief, he's also a recovering addict who's been sober for the past fifteen years. The father of two boys, Elijah, twenty-four, and Elvis, eighteen months, Bob lives with his wife and baby in Los Angeles, California.

Michael Albo is a Los Angeles–based author and journalist who has written about popular culture and true crime. He is a regular contributor to *LA Weekly* and the *Los Angeles Times*. His work has also appeared in the *Chicago Tribune*, *Premiere* magazine, *Men's Edge* magazine, and the music magazine *Sonic Boomers*. His short story "Baby, I Need to See a Man About a Duck" appears in the book *The Heroin Chronicles*.